Children of Harford County Maryland

Indentures and Guardianships

1801-1830

Henry C. Peden, Jr.

HERITAGE BOOKS
2008

HERITAGE BOOKS
AN IMPRINT OF HERITAGE BOOKS, INC.

Books, CDs, and more—Worldwide

For our listing of thousands of titles see our website
at
www.HeritageBooks.com

Published 2008 by
HERITAGE BOOKS, INC.
Publishing Division
100 Railroad Ave. #104
Westminster, Maryland 21157

Originally published 1994

International Standard Book Numbers
Paperbound: 978-1-58549-295-4
Clothbound: 978-0-7884-7152-0

FOREWORD

This book pertains to children of Harford County, Maryland who were indentured and/or appointed guardians, between 1801 and 1830. The information was gleaned from General Entries Books, 1801-1830. These records are available in the Register of Wills Office in Bel Air, Maryland and the Maryland State Archives in Annapolis, Maryland.

Indentures and guardianships are two important sources for genealogical information, especially since they name the children (and orphans), parents (one or both, sometimes neither), and the ages or dates of birth of the children (in most cases). They also may contain other useful data such as the places of residence, the names of other relatives, and occupations. Most indentures usually lasted until the boys reached age 21 and the girls reached age 16, during which time they faithfully served their masters in exchange for learning a trade and receiving schooling. Many were indentured simply to "learn to read, write and cipher to the rule of three." At the end of their servitude they were given their freedom and a set of clothes was oftentimes provided. As was typical during the times, most boys learned a trade or craft while the girls performed "housewifery." If they misbehaved during their indenture (such as running away) they could end up serving longer to make up for their lost time.

In addition to these indenture records one should also consult all available guardianship accounts and other probate records for additional data on their families of interest. Other books by the author will prove useful in this regard, namely: *Abstracts of the Orphans Court Proceedings, 1778-1800*, *Heirs and Legatees of Harford County, 1774-1802*, *Heirs and Legatees of Harford County, 1802-1846*, *Early Harford Countians* (which covers the years 1773 through 1790), and *Revolutionary Patriots of Harford County, Maryland, 1775-1783*. All of these books are available through Family Line Publications. Shirley Reightler's *Illegitimate Children of Harford County, 1800-1900* will also prove interesting. Since Harford County was formed from Baltimore County in 1773 and its governmental records begin in March, 1774, one should consult Baltimore County records for their Harford County lines prior to that time.

Henry C. Peden, Jr.
Bel Air, Maryland
May 1, 1994

AARON (Negro), age 5 on November 1, 1815, was indentured to John
Watkins in 1815 to learn to be a farmer.

ABRAHAM (Negro), age 7 on June 15, 1808, was indentured as a
servant to Joseph Robinson in 1808.

ABRAHAM (Negro), age 7 on May 1, 1819, was indentured to John
McComas in 1819 to learn to be a cooper.

ABRAHAM (Negro), age 11 years and 8 months in August, 1823, was
indentured with the consent of his mother (not named) to
William Wallis to learn to be a farmer.

ABRAHAM (Negro), age 8 in February, 1806, was indentured to David
Maulsby in 1806 to learn to be a farmer.

ABRAHAM (Negro), age about 43 in 1823, valued at $350, and
formerly owned by William Calwell, deceased, in October, 1823.

ABRAHAM, JR. (Negro), age about 6 in 1823, valued at $100, and
formerly owned by William Calwell, deceased, in October, 1823.

ACHES, ISAAC, age 16 on August 2, 1822, was indentured with the
consent of his mother (not named) to John A. Webster in 1821
to learn to be a seaman.

ADAMS, JOHN (orphan), age 16 on November 9, 1825, was indentured
to Robert Patterson in 1826 to learn to be a blacksmith.

ADAMS, SAMUEL (alias BENNINGTON), illegitimate son of Abigail
Bennington, age 8 in 1809, was indentured with the consent of
his mother to Jacob Balderston on June 24, 1809.

ADAMS, SAMUEL (Negro), age 8 on April 17, 1814, was indentured
with the consent of his mother (not named) to Alexander
McComas in 1814 to learn to be a farmer.

ADAMS, WILLIAM, master of William Singleton in 1813 indenture.

ADELINE (Negro), age 11 in January, 1812, was indentured to
Thomas and Clarissa Shay in 1812 to learn to do housework.

ADY, CLOE, age 15 in 1808. Court appointed Solomon Ady as her
guardian in August, 1808.

ADY, SOLOMON, guardian of Cloe Ady in 1808.

AILES, SAMUEL, master of Eanus Scarborough in 1817 indenture.

ALDERSON, ABEL, guardian of Corbin Amos in 1827.

ALDRIDGE, GILBERT, age 14 in June 20, 1802, was indentured to
Israel Bowman in 1802 to learn to be a chair maker.

ALEXANDER, JAMES, master of Elias Norrington in 1808 indenture.

ALLEN, JAMES, age 13 on November 15, 1800, was indentured to ----
[name illegible] in 1801 to learn to be a joiner.

ALLEN, JOHN, master of Negro Freeborn in 1802 indenture.

ALLEN, THOMAS (orphan), age 11 on August 15, 1828, was indentured
to Henry Bowman, Jr. in 1829 to learn to be a cooper.

ALLEN, WILLIAM, guardian of John G. Hill in 1816.

ALLENDER, ELIHU, master of Samuel Hudson in 1809 indenture,

ALLENDOFFER, ELIZABETH, age 7 on July 1, 1815, was indentured to
Mathew Hawkins in 1815 to learn to do housework.

ALLENDOFFER, WILLIAM (orphan), age 6 on August 1, 1816, was
indentured to Joseph H. Coale in 1813 to learn to be a farmer.

ALLISON, JOSEPH, age 12 on May 13, 1818, was indentured with the
consent of his mother (not named) to John Boyd, Jr. in 1819 to
learn to be a cordwainer.

AMEA (Negro), age 13 on August 31, 1812, was indentured with the consent of her mother (not named) to Isaiah and Mary Roberts to learn to do housework.

AMOS, CORBIN, age 16 on March 26, 1826. Court appointed Abel Alderson as his guardian on January 23, 1827.

AMOS, JAMES, master of Nancy Nowrey in 1806 indenture.

AMOS, OLIVER H., master of Ralph Williams and Benjamin Williams (colored sons of William Williams) in 1828 indenture.

AMOS, PHILLIP, master of Mary Morrison in 1826.

AMOSS, ANN MARIA, age 9 on October 10, 1815. Court appointed Susanna Amoss as her guardian in 1816.

AMOSS, JAMES (son of William Amoss), master of Joshua West in 1803 indenture.

AMOSS, JAMES, master of Negro Harry (orphan) in 1816 indenture.

AMOSS, JAMES, master of Negro James (orphan) in 1819 indenture.

AMOSS, JAMES McCOMAS (orphan), age 16 on May 21, 1830, was indentured by his own consent to Thomas Hanway in 1830 to learn the carding, spinning, weaving and dressing of cloth.

AMOSS, LEVI (son of Zachariah Amoss), age 18 on September 12, 1814, was indentured to Joseph Ashton in 1813 to learn to be a blacksmith.

AMOSS, LEVI, age 20 on September 12, 1815. Court appointed Susanna Amoss as his guardian in 1816.

AMOSS, PHILIP, age 19 on March 18, 1816. Court appointed Susanna Amoss as his guardian in 1816.

AMOSS, SUSANNA, age 11 on August 11, 1815. Court appointed Susanna Amoss as her guardian in 1816.

AMOSS, SUSANNA, guardian of Levi Amoss, Philip Amoss, Susanna Amoss and Ann Maria Amoss in 1816.

AMOSS, WILLIAM (son of Thomas Amoss), master of William Morris (Negro) in 1818 indenture.

AMOSS, WILLIAM, father of James Amoss in 1803 indenture.

AMOSS, WILLIAM, guardian of Samuel Richardson and Thomas Richardson in 1819.

AMOSS, WILLIAM LEE, master of Thomas Chambers (Negro) in 1822 indenture.

AMOSS, WILLIAM, master of Adaline Black (Negro) in 1818 indenture.

AMOSS, WILLIAM, master of Amos Prine in 1828 indenture.

AMOSS, ZACHARIAH, father of Levi Amoss in 1813 indenture.

AMY (Negro), mother of free Negro Asbury Wilson in 1807 indenture.

ANDERSON, JOHN, master of Charles Thompson in 1811 indenture.

ANDERSON, JOHN, master of Edward Saunders and William Saunders in 1814 indenture.

ANDREWS, ELBRIDGE (son of Capt. William Andrews, of Baltimore City), age 14 on February 14, 1828, was indentured to Robert W. Bolton, of Abingdon, Maryland, in 1828 to learn to be a hatter.

ANDREWS, FREDERICK (son of Capt. William Andrews, of Baltimore City), age 15 on April 21, 1828, was indentured to Robert W. Bolton, of Abingdon, Maryland, in 1828 to learn to be a hatter.

ANDREWS, JOHN, age 16 on May 16, 1808, formerly indentured to Thomas Sampson, now deceased, was indentured to Parker Gilbert in 1808 to learn to be a tailor.

ANDREWS, JOHN, age 10 on May 16, 1802, was indentured to Thomas Sampson in 1802 to learn to be a weaver.

ANDREWS, WILLIAM (Captain, of Baltimore City), father of Elbridge Andrews and Frederick Andrews in 1828 indentures.

AQUILLA (Mulatto), age 16 in February, 1811, was indentured to Thomas Shay in 1812 to learn to be a farmer.

ARCH (Negro orphan), age 12 on November 19, 1826, was indentured to Edward M. Chew in 1827 to learn to be a farmer.

ARCHER, JAMES P., no age given in 1824. Court appointed Stevenson Archer as his guardian in April, 1824.

ARCHER, JOHN, age 15 on April 9, 1824. Court appointed Dr. Robert Archer as his guardian in 1824.

ARCHER, ROBERT (Doctor), guardian of Robert H. Archer and John Archer in 1824.

ARCHER, ROBERT H., age 13 in 1824. Court appointed Dr. Robert Archer as his guardian in 1824.

ARCHER, STEVENSON, guardian of James P. Archer in 1824.

ARMONT, ANN, deceased mother of James Armont in 1806 indenture.

ARMONT, JAMES (son of James Cook and Ann Armont, both deceased), age 13 on March 1, 1806, was indentured with the consent of his aunt, Mary Armont, on February 22, 1806, to John S. Peck & Co. to learn to be a tanner.

ARMONT, MARY, aunt of James Armont in 1806 indenture.

ARMSTRONG, HANNAH, guardian of Martha Perine and Nimrod Perine in 1801.

ARMSTRONG, HANNAH, guardian of James Kimble, John Kimble, Stephen Kimble, and Meranda Kimble in 1813.

ARNOLD, WILLIAM, master of Samuel Pritchard in 1802 indenture.

ASELTON, STEPHEN (orphan), age 13 in May, 1808, was indentured to Morris Malsby in 1809 to learn to be a blacksmith.

ASHMORE, JOHN, master of Margaret Davis in 1819 indenture.

ASHTON, JOHN, master of Negro Fanny (daughter of Negro Priss) in 1804 indenture.

ASHTON, JOSEPH, master of George Dawson in 1810 indenture.

ASHTON, JOSEPH, master of Levi Amoss in 1814 indenture.

ASHTON, RICHARD, master of William Everett in 1806 indenture.

AUSTIN, COLEGATE (son of Martha and John Austin, Jr.), age 15 on March 23, 1817. Court appointed Thomas Jay as his guardian in 1817.

AUSTIN, EDWARD (son of Martha and John Austin, Jr.), age 17 on February 2, 1817. Court appointed Thomas Jay as his guardian in 1817.

AUSTIN, ESTHER (daughter of Martha and John Austin, Jr.), age 10 on "January or March 17, 1817." Court appointed Thomas Jay as her guardian in 1817.

AUSTIN, GEORGE (son of Martha and John Austin, Jr.), age 19 on May 22, 1817. Court appointed Thomas Jay as his guardian in 1817.

AUSTIN, JOHN JR., see "Martha and John Austin, Jr.," q.v., in 1817.

AUSTIN, MARTHA AMD JOHN JR., parents of George Austin, Edward Austin, Colegate Austin, and Esther Austin in March, 1817, by which time John Austin, Jr. was deceased.

AVARILLA (Negro), age 12 in April, 1808, was indentured to

Alexander Hannah in 1808 to learn to do housework.

AYRES, AMELIA, mother of Jarrett Ayres in 1815 indenture.

AYRES, AQUILA (alias DAVISON), age 11 on January 29, 1802, was indentured to Robert Taylor in 1801 to learn to be a cordwainer.

AYRES, AQUILA (alias DAVISON), age 16 on January 29, 1807, was indentured to John Dougherty to learn to be a farmer.

AYRES, JARRETT, age 18 on June 15, 1815, was indentured with the consent of his mother, Amelia Ayres, to Jacob Gilbert in 1815 to learn to be a house carpenter.

AYRES, THOMAS, master of Samuel Garrett in 1817 indenture.

AYRES, THOMAS SR., guardian of Luther Hitchcock, Jarrett Hitchcock, and Dennis Hitchcock in 1818.

BAGLEY, JOHN ORRICK, master of Negro Gerrard in 1828 indenture.

BAILEY, GERRARD, age 16 on May 22, 1811, was indentured with the consent of his mother, Rachel Bailey, to John Tucker in 1811 to learn to be a carpenter.

BAILEY, RACHEL, mother of Gerrard Bailey in 1811 indenture.

BAILEY, ZEPHANIAH, master of Nat Stokes (Negro) in 1806 indenture.

BAKER, GEORGE (son of Gideon Baker), age 18 on February 14, 1811, was indentured to James Paca in 1811 to learn to be a shoemaker.

BAKER, GIDEON, father of George Baker in 1811 indenture.

BALDERSTON, JACOB, master of Samuel Adams (alias Bennington) in 1809 indenture.

BALDWIN, NICHOLAS, age 18 on May 4, 1808, was indentured to William Spencer in 1809 to learn to be a shoemaker.

BANKHEAD, JOHN, master of Elenor Black in 1825 indenture.

BARCLAY, JOHN (son of John Barclay), age 19 on July 18, 1828, was indentured to John Morrison in 1828 to learn to be a cordwainer.

BARCLAY, JOHN, father of John Barclay in 1828 indenture.

BARCLAY, ROBERT, age 17 on October 14, 1807, was indentured with the consent of his mother (not named) to John Caldwell in 1808 to learn to be a cabinet maker.

BARCLAY, ROBERT, master of Reuben Forwood in 1814 indenture.

BARNES, AMOS, age 16 on July 5, 1808, was indentured with the consent of his mother, Mary Barnes, to Parker Gilbert in 1808 to learn to be a tailor.

BARNES, BENNET, guardian of Sarah Barnes, John Barnes, and Garrett Barnes in 1802.

BARNES, BENNET, no age given in 1826. Court appointed Aquila Brown as his guardian on December 5, 1826.

BARNES, BENNETT, guardian of Mary Barnes and Lydia Barnes in 1810.

BARNES, FORD, father of Mary Barnes and Lydia Barnes in 1810 indenture.

BARNES, GARRETT (orphan), age 15 on February 8, 1804, was indentured to Parker Gilbert in 1804 to learn to be a taylor.

BARNES, GARRETT, age 13 on February 8, 1802. Court appointed Bennet Barnes as his guardian in 1802.

BARNES, JOHN, age 19 on March 1, 1802. Court appointed Bennet Barnes as his guardian in 1802.

BARNES, JOHN R., no age given in 1826. Court appointed Aquila

Brown as his guardian on December 5, 1826.

BARNES, LYDIA (daughter of Ford Barnes), age 1 on August 25, 1810. Court appointed Bennett Barnes as her guardian in 1810.

BARNES, MARY (daughter of Ford Barnes), age 3 on October 6, 1810. Court appointed Bennett Barnes as her guardian in 1810.

BARNES, MARY, mother of Amos Barnes in 1808 indenture.

BARNES, RICHARD, master of Samuel Bowser (Negro) in 1808 indenture.

BARNES, SARAH, age 15 on August 22, 1801. Court appointed Bennet Barnes as her guardian in 1802.

BARNES, THOMAS, master of John Davis (son of Robert Davis) in 1816 indenture.

BARNES, WILLIAM (orphan), age 16 on September 28, 1804, was indentured to William McJilton in 1805 to learn to be a shoemaker.

BARNES, WILLIAM, age 14 in 1803. Court appointed Samuel Bay as his guardian in 1803.

BARNES, WILLIAM, age 17 in 1806. Court appointed Aquila Massey as his guardian in 1806 "in room of Samuel Rea who left this state."

BARNETT, HESTER (daughter of Joseph Barnett, deceased), age 9 in August, 1803. Court appointed James Barnett as her guardian in 1804.

BARNETT, JAMES (son of Joseph Barnett, deceased), age 12 in March, 1804. Court appointed James Barnett as his guardian in 1804.

BARNETT, JAMES, guardian of Hester Barnett, James Barnett, and Joanna Barnett in 1804.

BARNETT, JOANNA (daughter of Joseph Barnett, deceased), age 6 in April, 1804. Court appointed James Barnett as her guardian in 1804.

BARNETT, JOSEPH, deceased father of Hester Barnett, James Barnett, and Joanna Barnett in 1804 guardianship.

BARNETT, Thomas, master of Margaret Burk in 1803 indenture.

BARTOL, BARNEY B., age 1 in October, 1806. Court appointed Nancy Bartol as his guardian in 1807.

BARTOL, ELIZABETH, age 11 in October, 1806. Court appointed Nancy Bartol as her guardian in 1807.

BARTOL, GEORGE, age 13 in December, 1806. Court appointed Nancy Bartol as his guardian in 1807.

BARTOL, GEORGE, master of John McLaughlin in 1808 indenture.

BARTOL, HARRIOT, age 4 in June, 1806. Court appointed Nancy Bartol as her guardian in 1807.

BARTOL, MARY ANN, age 6 in September, 1806. Court appointed Nancy Bartol as her guardian in 1807.

BARTOL, NANCY, guardian of George Bartol, Elizabeth Bartol, Mary Ann Bartol, Harriot Bartol, and Barney B. Bartol in 1807.

BAY, HUGH, master of Mary Norrington in 1804 indenture.

BAY, JOHN, master of Thomas Blaney and Ann Blaney in 1821 indenture.

BAY, SAMUEL, guardian of William Barnes in 1803.

BAY, WILLIAM, master of Phebe Nevill in 1824 indenture.

BAYELY, SAMUEL H., master of Negro Harriot in 1824 indenture.

BAYLESS, ELIZABETH, guardian of John B. Bayless and Martha Bayless in 1802.

BAYLESS, HARRIOTT, age 14 in September, 1801. Court appointed
Thomas Jeffery as her guardian in 1802.

BAYLESS, JAMES, age 13 in 1803. Court appointed Thomas Jeffery as
his guardian in 1803.

BAYLESS, JOHN B., guardian of Edward Presbury, Septimus Presbury,
Sophia Presbury, Ellen Presbury, and Octavius Presbury in
1827.

BAYLESS, JOHN BROWN, age 14 on October 17, 1802. Court apointed
Elizabeth Bayless as his guardian in 1802.

BAYLESS, MARTHA, age 11 on December 6, 1801. Court appointed
Elizabeth Bayless as her guardian in 1802.

BAYLESS, NATHANIEL, age 10 on March 15, 1803. Court appointed
Lemuel Kenly as his guardian in 1803.

BAYLESS, WILLIAM, age 18 on April 6, 1818. Court appointed
Zepheniah Bayless as his guardian in 1818.

BAYLESS, ZEPHENIAH, guardian of William Bayless in 1818.

BEATON, MARGARET ANN, age 10 on October 8, 1829, was indentured
to Joseph Trimble in 1830 to learn to spin, sew and do other
housewifery.

BEAUMONT, MIFLIN, master of Edward Hamilton in 1822 indenture.

BEAVER, ELIZABETH (orphan), age 8 in September, 1815, was
indentured to Joseph Davis in 1815 to learn to do housework.

BEAVIN, BAKER (son of Charles Beavin), age 21 on September 7,
1810[?], was indentured to Cornelius Walker, of Baltimore
County, in 1803, to learn to be a slater and plasterer.

BEAVIN, CHARLES, father of Baker Beavin in 1803 indenture.

BELL, JAMES LUCKY, age 15 on August 6, 1807. Court appointed
Thomas Jeffery as his guardian in 1808.

BELL, JOHN BOYD, age 19 on April 3, 1808. Court appointed Thomas
Jeffery as his guardian in 1808.

BELL, REBECCA COCHRAN, age 13 on October 4, 1807. Court appointed
Thomas Jeffery as her guardian in 1808.

BELL, WILLIAM, master of Anthony Gover (Negro) in 1809 indenture.

BEMIS, NATHAN L., master of William Traplin in 1822 indenture.

BEN (Negro), age 7 on August 20, 1802, was indentured to Thomas
Taylor (ship carpenter) in 1803 to learn to be a farmer.

BEN (Negro), age 9 on April 1, 1811, was indentured to Dr. Thomas
E. Bond in 1811 to learn to be a farmer.

BENDLE, BENJAMIN, no age given in February, 1821, was indentured
with the consent of his mother, Margaret Bendle, to William
Bradford in 1821 to learn to be a hatter.

BENDLE, MARGARET, mother of Benjamin Bendle in 1821 indenture.

BENJAMIN (Negro), age 9 on February 28, 1829, was indentured to
Pheba Morgan in 1829 to learn to be a farmer.

BENJAMIN (Negro), age 6 on March 1, 1816, was indentured to
Penseld Kidd in 1816 to learn to be a farmer.

BENJAMIN (Negro), age 2 on May 5, 1808, was indentured to David
Tate in 1808.

BENNET, PHILIP, master of John Whitaker in 1808 indenture.

BENNINGTON, ABIGAIL, mother of Samuel Adams (alias Bennington) in
1809 indenture.

BENNINGTON, JEREMIAH, master of James Norris in 1822 indenture.

BENNINGTON, SAMUEL, see "Samuel Adams (alias Bennington)," q.v.,
in 1809.

BENSON, JOEL, age 3 on August 26, 1818. Court recognized Mary

Benson as his mother and guardian in 1818.

BENSON, JOEL, no age given in 1824. Court appointed Ralph S. Lee as his guardian in 1824.

BENSON, MARY, mother and guardian of Joel Benson in 1818.

BETTY (Negro), age about 40 in 1823, valued at $120, and formerly owned by William Calwell, deceased, in October, 1823.

BEVARD, GEORGE, master of Washington Bevard in 1822 indenture.

BEVARD, JOHN, master of William Chancey and Madison Ford in 1827 indentures.

BEVARD, WASHINGTON (orphan), age 13 on July 27, 1822, was indentured to George Bevard in 1822 to learn to be a cooper.

BIDDISON, JEREMIAH, guardian of William Strong and Elinor Strong in 1803.

BILL (Negro), age 10 in September, 1821, was indentured to Joseph Davis, Sr. to learn to be a farmer.

BILLINGSLEA, ELIZABETH, guardian of Susanna Billingslea and Sarah Billingslea in 1826.

BILLINGSLEA, JACOB (Negro), age 11 on November 1, 1828, was indentured with the consent of his father (not named) to John Bowman in 1828 to learn to be a farmer.

BILLINGSLEA, SARAH, age 16 in September, 1825, chose Elizabeth Billingslea as her guardian in 1826.

BILLINGSLEA, SUSANNA, age 20 on December 4, 1825, chose Elizabeth Billingslea as her guardian in 1826.

BIRCKHEAD, CHARLOTTE, was recognized by the Court as the natural guardian of James Wetherall, Henry Wetherall, Thomas Nicholson G. Wetherall, William Wetherall, and Matthew Wetherall in 1816.

BIRCKHEAD, THOMAS H., guardian of John Watters in 1807.

BLACK, ADALINE (Negro), age 2 years and 6 months on November 1, 1818, was indentured with the consent of her mother (not named) to William Amoss in 1818 to learn to do housework.

BLACK, ELENOR (daughter of Samuel Black), no age given in 1825, was indentured to John Bankhead for 12 years and 8 months from February 15, 1825, to learn to do housework.

BLACK, SAMUEL, father of Elenor Black in 1825 indenture.

BLACK, SAMUEL, father of Elenor Black in 1824 indenture.

BLANEY, ANN, age 14 in December, 1821. Court appointed John Bay as her guardian in 1821.

BLANEY, PATTY, age 14 on December 14, 1811. Court appointed Thomas St. Clair as her guardian in 1812.

BLANEY, THOMAS, age 16 in December, 1821. Court appointed John Bay as his guardian in 1821.

BODDEN, JOANNA, age 9 on March 30, 1818, was indentured with the consent of her mother (not named) to David Tucker in 1819 to learn to do housework.

BODDEN, MARY ANN, age 6 on August 5, 1819, was indentured with the consent of her mother (not named) to Thomas Scott in 1819 to learn to do housework.

BOID, ALEXANDER, master of Edward McCowen in 1822 indenture.

BOLTON, ROBERT W., master of Elbridge Andrews and Frederick Andrews in 1828 indentures.

BOND, BUCKLER, master of Negro William in 1803 indenture.

BOND, CAIPHUS (Negro), age 10 on May 10, 1822, was indentured to Thomas Mather in 1822 to learn to be a farmer.

BOND, ELIJAH M., age 10 on December 2, 1810. Court appointed Mary Bond as his guardian in 1811.

BOND, HARRY (Negro), son of Ned Bond (Negro), age 17 on October 4, 1820, was indentured to Benjamin Gibson in 1819 to learn to be a cooper.

BOND, JOHN (orphan), age 18 on February 12, 1808, was indentured to John Jackson in 1808 to learn to be a house carpenter.

BOND, JOSHUA J.[?], age 15 on March 4, 1816, was indentured to Samuel Richardson in 1816 to learn to clerk in the Register of Wills.

BOND, MARY, guardian of Nicholas M. Bond and Elijah M. Bond in 1811.

BOND, MEREKIN, guardian of James Wilmer in 1810.

BOND, NED (Negro), father of Harry Bond (Negro) in 1819 indenture.

BOND, NICHOLAS M., age 13 on May 23, 1810. Court appointed Mary Bond as his guardian in 1811.

BOND, SARAH, master of Rachel Toogood (Negro) in 1804 indenture.

BOND, SARAH, mother and guardian of Susannah Bond in 1804.

BOND, SUSANNAH (daughter of Sarah Bond), age 13 on June 31 [sic], 1804. Court appointed Sarah Bond as her guardian in 1804.

BOND, THOMAS, by his 1800 will, freed Negro Mary when she became age 25 [but it was not recorded until 1829 when she was age 35].

BOND, THOMAS E. (Doctor), master of Negro Tom, Negro Ben, and Negro Solomon in 1811.

BOND, THOMAS W., guardian of Catherine S. Nabb in 1815.

BOSLEY, DANIEL, guardian of Elizabeth Crawford, James Crawford, Daniel Crawford, Robert Crawford, and William Crawford in 1816.

BOSLEY, JOSEPH, master of Michael Murry in 1823 indenture.

BOSLEY, WILLIAM, age 11 on June 24, 1811, was indentured with the consent of his mother (not named) to William Divers in 1811 to learn to be a cooper.

BOTTS, ISAEL [ASAEL], age 15 in 1803. Court appointed James Botts as his guardian in 1803.

BOTTS, JAMES, guardian of Isael [Asael] Botts in 1803.

BOTTS, WILLIAM (alias WELCH), an illegitimate child, age 17 on July 2, 1809, was indentured to John W. Crawford in 1809 to learn to be a blacksmith.

BOWEN, BENJAMIN, age 17 on March 20, 1806, was indentured with the consent of his father, Elisha Bowen, to John Caldwell in 1806 to learn to be a cabinet maker.

BOWEN, ELISHA, father of Benjamin Bowen in 1806 indenture.

BOWEN, ELISHA, father of Robert Bowen in 1811 indenture.

BOWEN, ROBERT (son of Elisha Bowen), no age given in December, 1811, was indentured to Samuel Dever in 1811 to learn to be a blacksmith.

BOWMAN, HENRY JR., master of Thomas Allen in 1829 indenture.

BOWMAN, ISRAEL, master of Gilbert Aldridge in 1802 indenture.

BOWMAN, JOHN, master of Jacob Billingslea (Negro) in 1828 indenture.

BOWSER, CHARLES H. (son of Grace Browser [sic], Negro), age 7 years and 10 months on November 2, 1826, was indentured to Thomas C. Stump in 1826 to learn to be a farmer.

BOWSER, SAMUEL (Negro), "illegitimate boy of color," age 12 in September, 1808, was indentured to Richard Barnes in 1808 to learn to be a waterman.

BOYD, ALEXANDER, see "Alexander Boid," q.v., in 1822.

BOYD, JOHN JR., master of Joseph Allison in 1819 indenture.

BOYD, STEPHEN, master of Rosana Washington in 1823 indenture.

BOYLES, DANIEL, age 11 years and 6 months on December 8, 1820, was indentured with the consent of his mother (not named) to John O'Neill in 1821 to learn to be a nail and spike maker.

BRADFORD, ABRAM (illegitimate child), age 9 on September 14, 1828, was indentured with the consent of his mother (not named) to Edward Thompson in 1828 to learn to be a farmer.

BRADFORD, BILL (Negro), age 9 in 1801, was indentured to John Ellis, Sr. in 1801 to learn to be a farmer.

BRADFORD, CHARLES (Negro), age 7 in 1801, was indentured to John Ellis, Jr. in 1801 to learn to be a farmer.

BRADFORD, DANIEL (Negro), age 10 on November 3, 1803, "his parents are out of the county," was indentured to Freeborn Brown in 1804 to learn to be a farmer.

BRADFORD, DANIEL, master of Chauncey Hollis in 1817 indenture.

BRADFORD, FLORA (Negro), mother of Henry Bradford (Negro) in 1818 indenture.

BRADFORD, GEORGE W., master of Benjamin Mackie in 1805 indenture.

BRADFORD, GEORGE W., master of Negro Sarah and Negro Ned in 1817 indenture.

BRADFORD, HENRY (Negro), age 10 on March 1, 1818, was indentured with the consent of his mother, Flora Bradford, of Baltimore County, to William Woodland (in Harford County) in 1818 to learn to be a farmer.

BRADFORD, JAMES (Negro), age 5 on June 30, 1802, was indentured with the consent of his mother (not named) to James and Comfort Madden in 1802 to learn to read and be a farmer.

BRADFORD, JENNY (Negro), age 4 on May 25, 1802, was indentured with the consent of her mother (not named) to James and Comfort Madden in 1802 to learn to read and do housework.

BRADFORD, JOHN P. (Negro orphan), age 12 on November 17, 1828, was indentured with the consent of his mother (not named) to James Orr in 1829 to learn to be a farmer.

BRADFORD, JOSEPH (Negro), age 14 on October 16, 1803, "his parents are out of the county," was indentured to Freeborn Brown in 1804 to learn to be a farmer.

BRADFORD, OMEIA (Negro), mother of Walter Bradford (Negro) in 1814 indenture.

BRADFORD, RICHARD (Mulatto), age 15 on May 25, 1821, was indentured with the consent of his mother (not named) to William B. Montgomery in 1821 to learn to be a farmer.

BRADFORD, ROBERT, master of Chauncey Hollis in 1817 indenture.

BRADFORD, SAMUEL, Esq., master of William Wright (Negro) in 1822 indenture.

BRADFORD, SAMUEL, master of Negro Priss in 1804 indenture.

BRADFORD, WALTER (Negro), age 9 on January 29, 1814, was indentured with the consent of his mother, Omeia Bradford (Negro), to Thomas Wilson in 1814 to learn to be a farmer.

BRADFORD, WILLIAM, guardian of William Osborn and Theadore Osborn in 1827.

BRADFORD, WILLIAM HENRY (Negro orphan), age 8 on June 5, 1828, was indentured with the consent of his mother (not named) to Henry Smith in 1828 to learn to be a farmer.

BRADFORD, WILLIAM, master of Jarret Brookman in 1828 indenture.

BRADFORD, WILLIAM, master of Benjamin Bendle and Absalom Brown in 1821 indentures.

BRADFORD, WILLIAM, master of Joseph Brooks, William Osborn, and Henry Maddon in 1826 indentures.

BRADFORD, WILLIAM, master of Henry Wetherall and William Ricketts in 1820 indentures.

BRADFORD, WILLIAM, of Abingdon, Maryland, master of Maximilian Strong in 1820 indenture.

BRADLEY, REBECCA, mother of Samuel Stallion [sic] in 1803 indenture.

BRADLEY, REBECCA, mother of orphan Samuel Stallions [sic] in 1804 indenture.

BRANNEN, RANDAL, age 17 on May 1, 1814, was indentured to Cyrus Courtney in 1813 to learn to be a harness maker.

BRANNON, JOHN, master of Negro Rhoda in 1827 indenture.

BRANSON, JOSHUA, master of William James in 1808 indenture.

BRANSON, OWEN, master of William Curry in 1811 indenture.

BRAZIER, HARRIET, age 8 in August, 1813, was indentured with the consent of her father (not named) to Morris Malsby to learn to do housework.

BRAZIER, JOHN (orphan), age 6 on May 5, 1828, was indentured to Jabez Kirkwood in 1828 to learn to be a blacksmith.

BREWER, JOHN, age 9 in 1821, was indentured to William Richardson, Sr. in 1821 to learn to be a farmer.

BRINDLEY, BENJAMIN, master of Benjamin Lukens in 1804 indenture.

BRINDLEY, NATHANIEL, master of Henry Singleton in 1822 indenture.

BROOK, JAMES, age 8 on March 16, 1814. Court appointed John Forwood as his guardian in 1815.

BROOK, JOHN, age 12 on October 12, 1814. Court appointed John Forwood as his guardian in 1815.

BROOK, SARAH, age 6 on February 8, 1814. Court appointed John Forwood as her guardian in 1815.

BROOKMAN, JARRET, age 17 on March 22, 1828, was indentured with the consent of his mother (not named) to William Bradford in 1828 to learn to be a hatter.

BROOKS, ABRAHAM, no age given in August, 1824, was indentured with the consent of his parents (not named, but Cato Brooks made his or her mark on this indenture) to Capt. John A. Webster until May 6, 1830, to learn seamanship.

BROOKS, CATO, probable parent of Abraham Brooks in 1824 indenture.

BROOKS, JOE (orphan), age 11 in October, 1822, was indentured to John Dallam in 1822 to learn to be a farmer.

BROOKS, JOHN (orphan), age 8 in December, 1822, was indentured to John Dallam in 1822 to learn to be a farmer.

BROOKS, JOHN, no age given in 1815, was indentured with the consent of his parents (not named) to James Tredway in April, 1815, to learn to be a cooper.

BROOKS, JOSEPH (orphan), age 14 on November 1, 1825, was indentured "with the consent of his friends" to William Bradford in 1826 to learn to be a hatter.

BROWN, ABSALOM (orphan), age 17 on March 5, 1821, was indentured to William Bradford in 1821 to learn to be a hatter.

BROWN, ABSALOM (son of Josiah Brown, deceased), age 18 in October, 1821. Court appointed Jesse Reynolds as his guardian in 1822.

BROWN, ABSALOM, age 12 in November, 1816. Court appointed Margaret Brown as his natural guardian in 1817.

BROWN, AQUILA, age 19 on April 6, 1812. Court appointed William Brown as his guardian in 1812.

BROWN, AQUILA, age 8 on April 12, 1801. Court appointed Susanna Brown as his guardian in 1801.

BROWN, AQUILA, guardian of Bennet Barnes and John R. Barnes in 1826.

BROWN, ELIZABETH, master of Susan Connolly in 1828 indenture.

BROWN, ELLWOOD, age 8 in November, 1816. Court appointed Margaret Brown as his natural guardian in 1817.

BROWN, ELWOOD (son of Josiah Brown, deceased), age 13 in October, 1821. Court appointed Jesse Reynolds as his guardian in 1822.

BROWN, FREEBORN, master of Daniel Bradford (Negro) and Joseph Bradford (Negro) in 1804.

BROWN, GARRETT, age 17 on June 11, 1811. Court appointed Jacob Brown as his guardian in 1811.

BROWN, JACOB, guardian of Garrett Brown, William Brown, and Mary Ann Brown in 1811.

BROWN, JOHN, age 14 on November 26, 1816. Court appointed Margaret Brown as his natural guardian in 1817.

BROWN, JOHN, master of Negro Henry in 1825 indenture.

BROWN, JOHN, master of Negro Henry in 1824 indenture.

BROWN, JOHN, master of Jefferson Dale in 1808 indenture.

BROWN, JOSEPH, age 17 on June 10, 1817. Court appointed Margaret Brown as his natural guardian in 1817.

BROWN, JOSIAH (son of Josiah Brown, deceased), age 13 in October, 1821. Court appointed Jesse Reynolds as his guardian in 1822.

BROWN, JOSIAH, age 10 in November, 1816. Court appointed Margaret Brown as his natural guardian in 1817.

BROWN, JOSIAH, deceased father of Absalom Brown, Josiah Brown, Elwood Brown, and Rachel Brown in 1822.

BROWN, MARGARET, was recognized by the Court as the natural guardian of Joseph Brown, John Brown, Absalom Brown, Josiah Brown, Ellwood Brown, and Rachel Brown in 1817.

BROWN, MARY, age 14 in 1801. Court appointed Susanna Brown as her guardian in 1801.

BROWN, MARY ANN, age 8 on November 2, 1810. Court appointed Jacob Brown as her guardian in 1811.

BROWN, RACHEL (daughter of Josiah Brown, deceased), age about 10 in October, 1821. Court appointed Jesse Reynolds her guardian in 1822.

BROWN, RACHEL, age 6 in November, 1816. Court appointed Margaret Brown as her natural guardian in 1817.

BROWN, SUSANNA, was appointed guardian of Mary Brown, William Brown, and Aquila Brown in 1801.

BROWN, THOMAS, master of John Heller in 1812 indenture.

BROWN, WILLIAM, age 13 on April 26, 1811. Court appointed Jacob Brown as his guardian in 1811.

BROWN, WILLIAM, age 14 in 1809, was indentured with the consent of his mother (not named) to James Greenfield in 1809 to learn to be a house carpenter.

BROWN, WILLIAM, age 10 on February 6, 1801. Court appointed Susanna Brown as his guardian in 1801.

BROWN, WILLIAM, guardian of Aquila Brown in 1812.

BROWNING, MARTHA, age 6 on January 1, 1803. Court appointed William Lester as her guardian in 1803.

BROWNING, MARTHA, age 10 on January 1, 1807. Court appointed John Monks as her guardian in 1807.

BROWNLEY, JOSEPH (Doctor), guardian of Thomas P. Forwood in 1817.

BRUCE, CHARLES F., age 8 on November 10, 1808, was indentured to James Kirk in 1809 to learn to be a weaver.

BRUSEBANKS, BENJAMIN, age 7 on April 4, 1806, was indentured with the consent of his mother (not named) to Thomas Sampson in 1806 to learn to be a weaver.

BRYARLY, ELIZABETH P. (daughter of Dr. Wakeman Bryarly), age 5 in December, 1820. Court appointed William D. Lee as her guardian in 1821.

BRYARLY, FAITHFUL, age 15 on March 27, 1803. Court appointed Margaret Bryarly as her guardian in 1804.

BRYARLY, ISABEL, age 13 on July 10, 1803. Court appointed Margaret Bryarly as her guardian in 1804.

BRYARLY, JAMES, guardian of Mary Bryarly in 1823.

BRYARLY, MARGARET, guardian of Faithful Bryarly, Isabel Bryarly and Samuel Bryarly in 1804.

BRYARLY, MARY, age 5 on October 15, 1823. Court appointed James Bryarly as her guardian in 1823.

BRYARLY, PRISCILLA E., by her will, freed Negro Frances and her mother Charlotte (Colored) on March 9, 1825.

BRYARLY, SAMUEL, age 17 on March 15, 1803. Court appointed Margaret Bryarly as his guardian in 1804.

BRYARLY, WAKEMAN (son of Dr. Wakeman Bryarly), age 10 months in August, 1821. Court appointed William D. Lee as his guardian in 1821.

BRYERLY, WAKEMAN (Doctor), master of Edward Presbury (Negro) in 1805.

BULL, BENNET, age 5 in June, 1806. Court appointed Sarah Bull as his guardian in 1806.

BULL, EDMOND, age 13 in June, 1806. Court appointed Sarah Bull as his guardian in 1806.

BULL, EDMOND, age 14 on June 22, 1807, was indentured with the consent of his mother, Sarah Bull, to John O'Danel in 1807 to learn to be a carpenter and joiner.

BULL, ELISHA, master of James Franklin Gibson in 1827 indenture.

BULL, ELISHA, master of John Bull in 1806 indenture.

BULL, JOHN, age 16 on February 16, 1806, was indentured with the consent of his mother (not named) to Elisha Bull in 1806 to learn to be a millwright.

BULL, JOHN, age 16 in February, 1806. Court appointed Sarah Bull as his guardian in 1806.

BULL, SARAH, guardian of John Bull, Edmond Bull, William Bull and Bennet Bull in 1806.

BULL, SARAH, mother of Edmond Bull in 1807 indenture.

BULL, WILLIAM, age 9 in February, 1806. Court appointed Sarah Bull as his guardian in 1806.

BULL, WILLIAM, guardian of Richard Ruff and Henry Ruff in 1810.

BULL, WILLIAM, master of Negro Solomon in 1803 indenture.

BURK, JAMES, father of William Burk, Morris Ingram Burk, and Margaret Burk in 1803 indenture.

BURK, MARGARET (daughter of James Burk), age 8 on March 26, 1803, was indentured to Thomas Barnett in 1803 to learn to be a housekeeper.

BURK, MORRIS INGRAM (son of James Burk), age 6 on February 22, 1803, was indentured to James Lytle in 1803 to learn to be a bootmaker.

BURK, WILLIAM (son of James Burk), age 4 on May 1, 1803, was indentured to Samuel Dinsmore in 1803 to learn to be a weaver.

BURKINS, JACOB, age 17 in March, 1804, was indentured to Thomas Kelly in 1804 to learn to be a cooper.

BURNETT, ASA, master of Samuel Jefferson Garrettson in 1818 indenture.

BURNS, WILLIAM, no age given in 1827, was indentured with the consent of his parents (not named) to George Gray for 5 years from June 8, 1827, to learn to be a boot and shoemaker.

BURRAS, THOMAS, age 14 on June 27, 1823, was indentured to James Madden in 1823 to learn to be a plasterer.

BUSSEY, HENRY G., master of Negro Richard in 1803 indenture.

BUSSEY, HENRY G., guardian of Sylvester Wheeler, Charles Wheeler, Augustin Wheeler, James Mitchell Wheeler, and Betsy Wheeler in 1811.

BUSSEY, HENRY G., guardian of Anna Wheeler and Julian Wheeler in 1809.

BUTLER, ELIAS (Negro), age 15 on November 1, 1820, was indentured with the consent of his mother (not named) to Ralph S. Lee in 1820 to learn to be a miller. [Same entry made in record in 1821].

BUTLER, ----[?], master of John Hill (Negro) and Sucky Hill (Negro) in 1802.

BYARD, JAMES (son of James Byard), age 16 on October 1, 1803, was indentured to William Cranan in 1804 to learn to be a cooper.

BYRNES, WILLIAM, master of William Chesney (alias Cain or Hughes) in 1819 indenture.

CAIN, ELIZABETH, guardian of Jane Cain in 1801.

CAIN, JANE, age 10 in January, 1802. Court appointed Elizabeth Cain as her guardian in 1801.

CAIN, JOHN, guardian of James Fickie and Ann Fickie in 1815.

CAIN, WILLIAM, see "William Chesney (alias Cain or Hughes)," q.v.

CALDER, JAMES, age 13 on December 10, 1816. Court recognized Naomi Renshaw as his natural guardian in 1817.

CALDER, JOHN, see "Naomi Renshaw," q.v., in 1817.

CALDER, LLOYD, age 11 on June 17, 1817. Court recognized Naomi Renshaw as his natural guardian in 1817.

CALDWELL, JOHN, master of Benjamin Bowen (son of Elisha Bowen) in 1806.

CALDWELL, JOHN, master of Robert Barclay in 1808.

CALWELL, JOHN, age 12 in November, 1815. Court appointed Thomas Calwell as his guardian in 1815.

CALWELL, LAURA ANN, age 3 in February, 1818. Court recognized Mary Calwell as her natural guardian in 1818.

CALWELL, MARY E., no age given in 1815. Court appointed Thomas

Calwell as her guardian in November, 1815.

CALWELL, MARY, natural guardian of Laura Ann Calwell in 1818.

CALWELL, SARAH E., age 14 in 1815. Court appointed Thomas Calwell as her guardian in November, 1815.

CALWELL, THOMAS, guardian of John Calwell, Sarah E. Calwell, William T. Calwell, and Mary E. Calwell in 1815.

CALWELL, WILLIAM, deceased by October 27, 1823, when his Negroes were valued as follows: Negro Linday (age 60, $30), Negro Abraham (age 43, $350), Negro Philip (age 27, $300), Negro Betty (age 40, $120), Negro Henry (age 17, $250), Negro Jefferson (age 15, $200), Negro Ned (age 12, $175), Negro Sophia (age 10, $100), Negro Sarah (age 8, $80), and Negro Abraham, Jr. (age 6, $100).

CALWELL, WILLIAM T., no age given in 1815. Court appointed Thomas Calwell as his guardian in November, 1815.

CANNON, JOHN, guardian of Noble Fie in 1816.

CANTLER, ROBERT (orphan), age 18 on May 9, 1829, was indentured to Joshua Stephens in 1829 to learn to be a stone mason.

CAREINS, WILLIAM, master of Thomas Shewell in 1811 indenture.

CAREINS, WILLIAM, master of Thomas Marsh in 1814 indenture.

CARLILE, JOHN FEDERAL WILLIAM, no age given in 1805. Court appointed William S. Dallam as his guardian in 1805.

CARMAN, ANDREW, father of Davis Carman in 1806 indenture.

CARMAN, DAVIS (son of Andrew Carman), no age given, was indentured to Amos McComas on October 16, 1805, to learn to be a blacksmith.

CARR, BENEDICT (Negro, illegitimate), age 10 on April 1, 1828, was indentured to Richard Farmer in 1828 to learn to be a farmer.

CARR, ROBERT, master of Jacob Hopkins (Negro) in 1802 indenture.

CARR, WILLIAM (illegitimate child), age 18 on February 25, 1822, was indentured to Benjamin Lukens in 1822 to learn to be a wheelwright.

CARROLL, BENJAMIN, father of Edward Perry Carroll in 1807 indenture.

CARROLL, EDWARD PERRY (son of Benjamin Carroll), age 17 on December 8, 1807, was indentured to Richard Thrift in 1807 to learn to be a cooper.

CARSINS, GEORGE, master of Frederic Swan in 1805 indenture.

CARSON, JOHN, age 11 on February 18, 1807, was indentured to Nathan Dean in 1807 to learn to be a miller.

CARTER, WILLIAM, age 16 on February 16, 1805, was indentured to Josias Scott McComas in 1806 to learn to be a hatter.

CARVER, JOSEPH C., master of William Kimball in 1829 indenture.

CESKY [?], ROBERT, master of Jupiter Dorsey (Negro) in 1829 indenture.

CHAMBERS, THOMAS (Negro), age 10 on July 4, 1822, "no parents in this county," was indentured to William Lee Amoss in 1822 to learn to be a farmer.

CHAMBERS, WILLIAM AND SARAH, guardians of Charlton Walthom, William Walthom, Sarah Elina Walthom, Thomas Walthom, and Philazanna Walthom in 1802.

CHANCE, CHARITY (Mulatto), age 4 on June 1, 1802, was indentured to Daniel Norris and Catherine his wife to learn to read the Bible.

CHANCE, CHARITY (Mulatto), age 6 on June 1, 1804, was indentured to Henry Woolsey to learn to do housework.

CHANCEY, WILLIAM (orphan), age 14 on August 12, 1827, was indentured to John Bevard in 1827 to learn to be a cooper.

CHANDLEE, THOMAS, master of Johannas Henry Crouse in 1814 indenture.

CHARLES (Negro), father of Negro Emanuel in 1802 indenture.

CHARLES (Negro), no age given in 1817, was indentured with the consent of his mother, Negro Sarah, to Cunningham Whiteford in November, 1817, to learn to be a farmer.

CHARLOTTE (Colored), age about 37 in 1825, and her daughter Frances, age about 1 year, were freed by the will of Priscilla E. Bryarly on March 9, 1825.

CHAUNCEY, GARRETT, guardian of Nester Chauncey and John Chauncey in 1809.

CHAUNCEY, GEORGE, guardian of Chauncey Webster and Caroline Webster in 1802.

CHAUNCEY, JOHN, age 19 on October 27, 1808. Court appointed Henry Vansickle as his guardian in 1809.

CHAUNCEY, JOHN, guardian of John H. Chauncey in 1818.

CHAUNCEY, JOHN H., age 8 on November 1, 1817. Court appointed John Chauncey as his guardian in 1818.

CHAUNCEY, NESTER, age 16 on March 21, 1809. Court appointed Garrett Chauncey as his guardian in 1809.

CHESNEY, ANNE, age 11 in April, 1827. Court appointed William Chesney as her guardian on March 12, 1828.

CHESNEY, JAMES, master of Richard Mitchell in 1822 indenture.

CHESNEY, WILLIAM (alias CAIN or HUGHES), age 18 on February 11, 1820, was indentured with the consent of his mother (not named) to William Byrnes in 1820 to learn to be a cooper.

CHESNEY, WILLIAM, guardian of Anne Chesney in 1828.

CHESNEY, WILLIAM, master of William Hamby in 1822 indenture.

CHEW, ANN W., mother of Daniel L. Chew and Eliza Cassandra Chew in 1819 guardianships.

CHEW, DANIEL L. (son of Ann W. Chew), age 5 on March 15, 1820. Court appointed William Worthington as his guardian in 1819.

CHEW, EDWARD M., master of Negro Arch in 1827 indenture.

CHEW, ELIJAH (Colored), age 10 on March 6, 1824, was indentured to John Coale in 1824 to learn to be a farmer.

CHEW, ELIZA CASSANDRA (daughter of Ann W. Chew), age 4 months on Janury 1, 1820. Court appointed William Worthington as her guardian in 1819.

CHEW, JACOB (free Negro son of Roger and Nelly Chew), age 13 years and 23 days on February 13, 1810, was indentured to John Jewett in 1810 to learn to be a farmer.

CHEW, ROGER AND NELLY, Negro parents of Jacob Chew in 1810 indenture.

CHEW, THOMAS, guardian of Thomas Chew Miller in 1801.

CHOCKE, JAMES, no age given in 1811, was indentured with the consent of his father (not named) to Aquila McComas in October, 1811, to learn to be a blacksmith.

CHOCKE, TUDOR, manumitted Negro Corbin and Negro Ruth in 1815.

CHRISTIE, CORDELIA P., guardian of Priscilla Hall Christie, Gabriel John Christie, Edward Christie, and Sarah Smith Christie in 1830.

CHRISTIE, EDWARD, age 9 on September 20, 1829. Court appointed
Cordelia P. Christie as his guardian in 1830.
CHRISTIE, GABRIEL JOHN, age 11 on October 28, 1829. Court
appointed Cordelia P. Christie as his guardian in 1830.
CHRISTIE, PRISCILLA HALL, age 13 in October, 1829. Court
appointed Cordelia P. Christie as her guardian in 1830.
CHRISTIE, SARAH SMITH, age 6 in February, 1830. Court appointed
Cordelia P. Christie as her guardian in 1830.
CLARK, ELIZABETH, age 11 on June 11, 1823, "having no living
parents," was indentured to James Fisher (son of Thomas
Fisher) in 1823 to learn to spin and sew.
CLENDENIN, JOHN, guardian of Mary Clendinen, Adam Clendinen, and
Amelia Clendinen (children of Adam Clendinen, deceased) in
1816.
CLENDINEN, ADAM (son of Adam Clendinen, deceased), born in
December, 1810. Court appointed John Clendenin [sic] as his
guardian in 1816.
CLENDINEN, AMELIA (daughter of Adam Clendinen, deceased), born in
October, 1812. Court appointed John Clendenin [sic] as her
guardian in 1816.
CLENDINEN, MARY (daughter of Adam Clendinen, deceased), born in
June, 1809. Court appointed John Clendenin [sic] as her
guardian in 1816.
COALE, JOHN, master of Elijah Chew (Colored) in 1824 indenture.
COALE, JOSEPH H., master of William Allendoffer (orphan) in 1813
indenture.
COALE, RICHARD, master of Samuel Seny[?] (Negro) in 1806
indenture.
COALE, SKIPWITH H., master of George Mays (Colored) in 1826
indenture.
COALE, SKIPWITH, master of Aaron Morings (Negro) in 1805
indenture.
COALE, WILLIAM, master of George Jordan (orphan) n 1825
indenture.
COATNEY, THOMAS, master of Henry Crangal in 1802 indenture.
COBY, JUDY (free Negro woman), mother of Negro boy Danby in 1808
indenture.
COCHRAN, JAMES, master of John Gallion in 1816 indenture.
COHEE, STEPHEN (orphan), age 13 on January 5, 1815, was
indentured to Abraham Midhalf in 1815 to learn to be a cart
and wagon maker.
COINE, SARAH (Colored), age 6 on March 2, 1830, was indentured to
Jane Herbert in 1829 to learn to be a housekeeper.
COLE, CORNELIUS, guardian of Susan Lytle, Benjamin Lytle, and
Joseph Lytle in 1821.
COLE, EDWARD (illegitimate child), age 8 on January 15, 1828, was
indentured with the consent of his mother (not named) to
William C. Kirkwood in 1828 to learn to be a farmer.
COLE, ELENNOR (Negro daughter of Mary Cole), age 6 on September
7, 1819, was indentured with the consent of her mother to
Robert Kerr in 1820 to learn to do housework.
COLE, ELIZA (orphan), age 12 on October 1, 1815, was indentured
to John Gibson in 1815 to learn to do housework.
COLE, ELIZABETH, age 13 on October 22, 1816. Court recognized
Sarah Cole as her natural guardian in 1817.

COLE, EMELA, age 5 on February 20, 1816. Court recognized Sarah
Cole as her natural guardian in 1817.

COLE, EZEKIEL, age 10 on August 12, 1816. Court recognized Sarah
Cole as his natural guardian in 1817.

COLE, JAMES COURTNEY, age 2 on April 22, 1816. Court recognized
Sarah Cole as his natural guardian in 1817.

COLE, JOHN AND PRISCILLA, guardians of Aquila Drew and Bennet
Drew in 1803.

COLE, JOHN WESLEY, age 2 on October 5, 1810. Court appointed Job
and Elizabeth Guest as his guardians in 1811.

COLE, JONAS COURTNEY, age 8 on February 20, 1816. Court
recognized Sarah Cole as his natural guardian in 1817.

COLE, MARY (Negro), mother of Elennor Cole (Negro) in 1820
indenture.

COLE, PRISCILLA AND JOHN, guardians of Aquila Drew and Bennet
Drew in 1803.

COLE, RICHARD, master of Negro Mary Ann in 1828 indenture.

COLE, SARAH, natural guardian of Elizabeth Cole, Ezekiel Cole,
Jonas Courtney Cole, William Cole, Emela Cole, and James
Courtney Cole in 1817.

COLE, WILLIAM (orphan), age 7 years, 7 months and 24 days on
August 31, 1816, was indentured to Ralph Sackett Lee in 1816
to learn to be a miller.

COLE, WILLIAM, age 6 on October 7, 1816. Court recognized Sarah
Cole as his natural guardian in 1817.

COLE, WILLIAM THOMAS, age 1 on January 6, 1811. Court appointed
Job and Elizabeth Guest as his guardian in 1811.

COLEMAN, FANNY (Negro), mother of Lewis Coleman (Negro) in 1828
indenture.

COLEMAN, LEWIS (Negro, son of Fanny), age 5 years and 5 months in
December, 1828, was indentured to Samuel Cox in 1828 to learn
to be a farmer.

COLLINS, ANN, mother of John and Harriott Collins in 1804
indenture.

COLLINS, HARRIOTT, age 5 on May 31, 1804, was indentured to John
and Margaret Douglass in 1804 to learn to do housework.

COLLINS, JOHN (son of Ann Collins), age 9 on July 1, 1804, was
indentured to John Douglass in 1804 to learn to be a weaver.

COLMAN, DAVID (Negro), father of Lunnon Colman in 1803 indenture.

COLMAN, LUNNON (Negro son of David Colman), no age given in 1803,
was indentured to Joshua Green in 1803 to learn to be a
farmer.

COMBEST, CYRUS, age 13 on May 5, 1806, was indentured to James
White in 1806 to learn to be a cartwright.

CONNELL, ELONER (illegitimate child), age 8 on June 15, 1811, was
indentured with the consent of her mother (not named) to Mary
Harry in 1811 to learn to do housework.

CONNELLY, JEREMIAH (orphan), age 14 on January 1, 1821, was
indentured to Abraham Heaps in 1820 to learn to be a
blacksmith.

CONNELLY, SAMUEL, master of Joshua Watters (Negro) in 1820
indenture.

CONNOLLY, SUSAN (orphan), age 8 years and 6 months on August 5,
1828, was indentured to Elizabeth Brown in 1828 to learn to do
housework.

COOK, HENRY (orphan), age 16 on May 2, 1823, was indentured to
James Hendon in 1822 to learn to be a cooper and a farmer.
COOK, JAMES, deceased father of James Armont in 1806 indenture.
COOK, SAMUEL (son of Samuel Cook, of Baltimore County), age 7 on
December 31, 1805, was indentured to Enos West, of Harford
County, in 1806 to learn to be a farmer.
COOLEY, CORBIN (son of Sarah Cooley), age 8 in August, 1807.
Court appointed Samuel Stephenson as his guardian in 1808.
COOLEY, DANIEL (son of Sarah Cooley), age 18 on March 24, 1808.
Court appointed Samuel Stephenson as his guardian in 1808.
COOLEY, ELIZABETH, guardian of John James Cooley in 1814.
COOLEY, JOHN JAMES, age 4 on October 16, 1813. Court appointed
Elizabeth Cooley as his guardian in 1814.
COOLEY, LAWSON (son of Sarah Cooley), age 6 in November, 1807.
Court appointed Samuel Stephenson as his guardian in 1808.
COOLEY, SARAH ANN (daughter of Sarah Cooley), age 3 in May, 1808.
Court appointed Samuel Stephenson as her guardian in 1808.
COOLEY, SARAH, mother of Daniel Cooley, Corbin Cooley, Lawson
Cooley, and Sarah Ann Cooley in 1808 indenture.
COOPER, ALEXANDER, age 17 in 1808, was indentured with the
consent of his father, John Cooper, to John Hawkins in 1808 to
learn to be a cartwright.
COOPER, JAMES, master of John Fisher in 1801 indenture.
COOPER, JOHN, father of Alexander Cooper in 1808 indenture.
CORBIN (Negro), age 12 on August 1, 1815, who was manumitted by
Tudor Chocke in Baltimore County indenture, was now indentured
to James Kennedy in 1815 to learn to be a farmer.
CORD, PROVIDENCE, no age given in 1816. Court appointed Edward
Timmons as her guardian in August, 1816.
CORDE, HENRY (Negro, illegitimate), age 15 on May 3, 1828, was
indentured to Christopher Wilson in 1828 to learn to be a
farmer.
CORSEY, JACOB (Negro), age 2 years and 9 months on May 15, 1821,
was indentured with the consent of his mother (not named) to
Elizabeth Cox, Jr. in 1821 to learn to be a farmer.
CORSHORN, JAMES, master of James C. Dawes in 1813 indenture.
COTRALL, WILLIAM, age 17 on February 9, 1801, was indentured to
James Fullerton in 1801 to learn to be a shoemaker.
COTTRALL, EPHRAIM (orphan), age 16 on March 12, 1803, was
indentured to James Fullerton in 1804 to learn to be a
cordwainer.
COTTS[?], SAMUEL, age 15 years and 9 months in June, 1807, was
indentured to Husband Hoale [sic] in 1807 [no trade or craft
listed].
COURTNEY, AMERICA, age 14 on February 24, 1824, was indentured
with the consent of his mother (not named) to William Hunter
in 1823 to learn to be a taylor.
COURTNEY, ANN MARIA, age 8 on March 13, 1801. Court appointed
Richard M. Taylor as her guardian in 1801.
COURTNEY, CYRUS, master of Randal Brannen in 1813 indenture.
COURTNEY, JOHN, guardian of James Osborn (son of William Osborn)
in 1806.
COURTNEY, THOMAS, see "Thomas Coatney," q.v., in 1802.
COVEY, JUDITH (Negro), mother of Sam Covey (Negro) in 1813
indenture.

COVEY, SAM (Negro), age 8 years, 5 months and 6 days on July 12, 1815 [sic], was indentured with the consent of his mother, Judith Covey (Negro), to William Finney in 1813 to learn to be a farmer.

COWAN, CHARITY (Negro daughter of Sam Cowan), age 11 in September, 1805, was indentured to Ralph Lee in 1806 to learn to do housework.

COWAN, SAM, father of Charity Cowan (Negro) in 1806 indenture.

COX, BAINES, master of Amos Currie (illegitimate child) in 1808 indenture.

COX, ELIZABETH JR., master of Jacob Corsey (Negro) in 1821 indenture.

COX, JAMES, age 11 in February, 1828, was indentured to Joseph Trimble in 1828 to learn to be a farmer.

COX, SAMUEL AND ELIZABETH, masters of Negro Melvina in 1822 indenture.

COX, SAMUEL, master of Lewis Coleman (Negro) in 1828 indenture.

COYE, JOHN (orphan), age 17 years and 6 months on January 1, 1828, was indentured to Joshua Stevens in 1828 to learn to be a stone mason.

CRANAN, WILLIAM, master of James Byard (son of James Byard) in 1804 indenture.

CRANGAL, BARTIS, father of Henry Crangal in 1802 indenture.

CRANGAL, HENRY (son of Bartis Crangal), age 17 on February 14, 1802, was indentured to Thomas Coatney [Courtney?] in 1802 to learn to be a carpenter and joiner.

CRAWFORD, DANIEL, age 9 in 1816. Court appointed Daniel Bosley as his guardian on October 3, 1816.

CRAWFORD, ELIZABETH, age 13 in 1816. Court appointed Daniel Bosley as her guardian on October 3, 1816.

CRAWFORD, JAMES, age 11 in 1816. Court appointed Daniel Bosley as his guardian on October 3, 1816.

CRAWFORD, JOHN, guardian of Parker Lee Crawford in 1814.

CRAWFORD, JOHN W., master of William Botts (alias Welch) in 1809 indenture.

CRAWFORD, PARKER LEE, no age given in 1814. Court appointed John Crawford as his guardian in November, 1814.

CRAWFORD, ROBERT, age 7 in 1816. Court appointed Daniel Bosley as his guardian on October 3, 1816.

CRAWFORD, WILLIAM, age 4 in 1816. Court appointed Daniel Bosley as his guardian on October 3, 1816.

CREIGE, HERMAN (orphan), age 14 in 1806, was indentured to George Robinson to learn to be a farmer.

CREVENSTEN, GEORGE, master of Joseph Everest Taylor and William Meeks in 1820 indentures.

CRISSEE, ROBERT, age 5 in June, 1826, was indentured with the consent of his father (not named) to John McFaddin in 1827 to learn to be a tailor.

CRISTY, WILLIAM (Negro orphan), age 5 on March 1, 1827, was indentured to John Hughes in 1828 to learn to be a farmer.

CRISWELL, ELIZABETH R. (daughter of George Criswell), age 11 on march 10, 1829, was indentured to John Judd in 1828 to learn to be a weaver.

CRISWELL, WILLIAM (illegitimate child), age 4 on February 1, 1805, was indentured with the consent of his mother (not named) to John Hanway in 1806 to learn to be a cooper.

CRISWELL, WILLIAM (orphan), age 8 on December 15, 1825, was indentured to Thomas McClure in 1825 to learn to be a tailor.

CRONIN, WILLIAM, master of Daniel McGonegall in 1808 indenture.

CROUSE, JOHANNAS HENRY (orphan), age 16 on January 25, 1814, was indentured to Thomas Chandlee in 1814 to learn to be a boot and shoemaker.

CUNNINGHAM, DANIEL, master of Aquila Scott McComas in 1817 indenture.

CUNNINGHAM, JOHN, master of "Negro or Mulatto" Mary Ann in 1809 indenture.

CUNNINGHAM, MORTIMORE, master of Eliza Jane Peck (Negro) in 1829.

CUNNINGHAM, MORTIMORE, master of Henry Hill (orphan) in 1825 indenture.

CUNNINGHAM, WALTER, no age given in 1821, was indentured with the consent of his father (not named) to John Moores and Aquila Paca Moores in November, 1821, to learn to be a tanner.

CURLEY, ELEANOR, age 12 on January 20, 1810. Court appointed Sarah Curley as her guardian in 1810.

CURLEY, HUGH, age 15 on May 6, 1809. Court appointed Sarah Curley as his guardian in 1810.

CURLEY, PATRICK, age 20 on September 8, 1809. Court appointed Sarah Curley as his guardian in 1810.

CURLEY, SARAH, guardian of Patrick Curley, Hugh Curley, and Eleanor Curley in 1810.

CURRIE, AMOS (illegitimate child), age 12 on February 28, 1807, was indentured to Baines Cox in 1808 to learn to be a farmer.

CURRY, AMOS (illegitimate child of Ann Curry), age 12 years and 15 days old on June 10, 1805, was indentured to Jonathan Smith in 1805 to learn to be a farmer.

CURRY, ANN, mother of Amos Curry (illegitimate son) in 1805 indenture.

CURRY, ARTHUR, father of William Curry in 1828 indenture.

CURRY, BENJAMIN (son of John Curry), age 15 on May 24, 1817, was indentured to John Price in 1816 to learn to be a cooper.

CURRY, JAMES, father of William Curry in 1811 and 1819 indentures.

CURRY, JOHN, father of Benjamin Curry in 1816 indenture.

CURRY, WILLIAM (son of Arthur Curry), age 16 on March 16, 1828, was indentured to James Daugherty in 1828 to learn to be a weaver.

CURRY, WILLIAM (son of James Curry), age 17 on February 14, 1819, was indentured to Vincent Jeffery in 1819 to learn to be a shoe and boot maker.

CURRY, WILLIAM (son of James Curry), no age given in 1811, was indentured to Owen Branson in February, 1811, to learn to be a farmer.

DALE, ANN, mother of Jefferson Dale in 1808 indenture.

DALE, JEFFERSON (son of Ann Dale), age 6 in May, 1808, was indentured with the consent of his mother to John Brown in 1808 to learn to be a cabinet maker.

DALLAM, JOHN, master of Joe Brooks and John Brooks (orphans) in 1823 indenture.

DALLAM, JOHN, master of Elizabeth Sarrah (an illegitimate child) in 1823 indenture.

DALLAM, RICHARD B., master of William Paca in 1804 indenture.
DALLAM, RICHARD B., master of James Wheeler in 1801 indenture.
DALLAM, WILLIAM, master of Negro Susannah in 1809 indenture.
DALLAM, WILLIAM S., guardian of John Federal William Carlile in 1805.
DANBY (Negro son of free woman Judy Coby), age 2 years, 7 months and 15 days on September 20, 1808, was indentured to James Thompson in 1808 to learn to be a farmer.
DAUGHERTY, ANN, master of Lucinda Quinlan in 1830 indenture.
DAUGHERTY, JAMES, master of William Curry in 1828 indenture.
DAUGHERTY, JOHN, master of Henry Oliver in 1819 indenture.
DAUGHERTY, JOHN, master of Daniel Ragan (orphan) in 1809 indenture.
DAVEY, JOHN, master of Samuel Stallions (orphan) in 1804 indenture.
DAVIS, JESSE (orphan), age 16 in January, 1805, was indentured to Stump & Price in 1805 to learn to be a miller.
DAVIS, JOHN (son of Robert Davis), age 16 on March 7, 1816, was indentured to Thomas Barnes in 1816 to learn to be a saddler.
DAVIS, JOHN, master of Vincent Jefferies (son of William Jefferies) in 1805 indenture.
DAVIS, JOHN, master of Abraham Long (son of John Long) in 1808 indenture.
DAVIS, JOSEPH, master of Elizabeth Beaver in 1815 indenture.
DAVIS, JOSEPH SR., master of Negro boy Bill in 1821 indenture.
DAVIS, MARGARET, age 12 on December 20, 1818, was indentured with the consent of her mother (not named) to John Ashmore in 1819 to learn to do housework.
DAVIS, REES, see "Reed & Davis," q.v.
DAVIS, ROBERT, father of John Davis in 1816 indenture.
DAVIS, WILEY (orphan), age 12 in September, 1815, was indentured to John Harvey in 1815 to learn to be a blacksmith.
DAVISON, AQUILA, see "Aquila Ayres (alias Davison)," q.v., in 1801.
DAWES, JAMES C., age 17 on December 7, 1813, was indentured with the consent of his father (not named) to James Corshorn in 1813 to learn to be a cartwright.
DAWSON, GEORGE (son of Thomas Dawson), age 15 on May 10, 1810, was indentured to Joseph Ashton in 1810 to learn to be a blacksmith.
DAWSON, THOMAS, father of George Dawson in 1810 indenture.
DAY, JAMES M., age 18 months on May 26, 1817. Court recognized Sarah Day as his natural guardian in 1817.
DAY, MILCHA, age 6 on May 25, 1817. Court recognized Sarah Day as her natural guardian in 1817.
DAY, PRISCILLA, age 4 on March 5, 1817. Court recognized Sarah Day as her natural guardian in 1817.
DAY, SARAH, natural guardian of Milcha Day, Priscilla Day, and James M. Day in 1817 indenture.
DEAN, NATHAN, master of John Carson in 1807 indenture.
DEAVER, HUGH, master of Negro Jack (son of Negro Mary) in 1805 indenture.
DEAVER, JAMES, master of Edward Morgan (Colored) in 1824 indenture.
DEAVER, MARTHA, mother of Sarah Deaver in 1806 indenture.

DEAVER, SARAH (daughter of Martha Deaver), no age given in 1806, was indentured with the consent of her mother to Mary Wilson to learn to do housework.

DEBRULAR, BENJAMIN (orphan), age 14 on October 1, 1802, was indentured to Ephraim Swart in 1803 to learn to be a wagon and cart maker or a wheelwright.

DEBRULAR, BENJAMIN (son of James Debrular), age 14 in 1803. Court appointed Jesse Taylor as his guardian in 1803.

DEBRULAR, CORDELIA, age 9 on September 29, 1801. Court appointed John Roberts as her guardian in 1802.

DEBRULAR, ELIZABETH, age 13 in 1802. Court appointed Charles Hipkins as her guardian in 1802.

DEBRULAR, JAMES, father of Benjamin Debrular in 1803 indenture.

DEMBY, MOSES (Negro son of Sarah Demby), age 2 on January 20, 1815, was indentured to John Weeks, Sr. in 1815 to learn to be a farmer.

DEMBY, SARAH (Negro), mother of Moses Demby (Negro) in 1815 indenture.

DEMPSEY, ELIZA (orphan), age 5 on August 15, 1803, was indentured to Enos West to learn to do housework.

DEMPSEY, ISAAC (orphan), age 14 on August 15, 1803, was indentured to Thomas West in 1804 to learn to be a farmer.

DENBOW, JOHN, guardian of Amelia and Mahalah Durham in 1805.

DENNISON, JOHN (son of William Dennison), age 10 on May 16, 1818, was indentured with the consent of his parents to John Millhoof in 1818 [no trade or craft listed].

DENNISON, WILLIAM, father of John Dennison in 1818 indenture.

DEVER, JOHN, master of Negro Jacob in 1825 indenture.

DEVER, JOHN, master of Negro John and Negro Washington in 1816 indentures.

DEVER, SAMUEL, master of Robert Bowen (son of Elisha Bowen) in 1811 indenture.

DEVOE, JOHN, master of John Smithson in 1805 indenture.

DICKSON, JOHN (illegitimate child of Rachel Dickson), age 15 years and 6 months in June, 1811, was indentured with the consent of his mother to John Morrison in 1811 to learn to be a shoemaker.

DICKSON, RACHEL, mother of John Dickson in 1811 indenture.

DINSMORE, SAMUEL, master of William Burk (son of James Burk) in 1803 indenture.

DITTO, ABRAHAM (orphan boy and son of Alisanna Russell), age 11 years, 7 months, and 26 days on November 9, 1805, was indentured to Joseph Wiggins in 1806 to learn to be a cabinet maker.

DIVER, ELIZABETH, master of Negro Mary Ann in 1816 indenture.

DIVERS, WILLIAM, master of William Bosley and John Gilmore in 1811 indentures.

DIVERS, WILLIAM, master of Negro Sam (orphan) in 1820 indenture.

DIVERS, WILLIAM, master of Lloyd Morris in 1803 indenture.

DIXON, JAMES HENRY (orphan), age 16 on August 30, 1830, was indentured with the consent of his grandfather (not named) to William G. Dove in 1830 to learn to be a farmer.

DOBBIN, JOHN, father of Robert Dobbin in 1830 indenture.

DOBBIN, ROBERT (son of John Dobbin), age 10 on June 3, 1830, was indentured with the consent of his father to Samuel Wilson in

1830 to learn to be a shoemaker.

DODDRELL, JAMES C., master of Henry Louis (Negro) in 1827 indenture.

DODDRELL, JAMES C., master of Sarah Taylor (Negro) and Samuel Weeks (Negro) in 1829 indentures.

DONAHO, DANIEL, father of James Thompson Donaho and William Henry Donaho in 1807 indentures.

DONAHO, JAMES THOMPSON (son of Daniel Donaho), age 14 on January 2, 1807, was indentured to Parker Gilbert in 1807 to learn to be a tailor.

DONAHO, WILLIAM HENRY (son of Daniel Donaho), age 7 on December 27, 1806, was indentured to Amos Gilbert in 1807 to learn to be a boot and shoemaker.

DONALDSON, MARY, mother of Henry Louis (Negro) in 1827 indenture.

DONN, JOHN (of Havre de Grace), master of George Mahan in 1803 indenture.

DOORAN, JOHN, guardian of Thomas Smithson, John Smithson, and Daniel Smithson in 1805.

DORAN, EDWARD, guardian of Philip Doran in 1819.

DORAN, JOHN, master of Eli Harry in 1818 indenture.

DORAN, PHILIP, age 11 on March 29, 1819. Court appointed Edward Doran as his guardian in 1819.

DORNEY, STEPHEN (illegitimate child), age 6 on February 18, 1806, was indentured with the consent of his mother (not named) to Timothy Keen in 1806 to learn to be a blacksmith.

DORNEY, THOMAS, guardian of Thomas Hipkins in 1828.

DORNEY, THOMAS, guardian of James L. Presbury in 1828.

DORSEY, GABRIEL (son of Josias Dorsey), age 13 on September 15, 1820, was indentured to William Stump in 1821 to learn to be a farmer.

DORSEY, GREENBERRY JR., age 18 in June, 1806. Court appointed John Wallis, Jr., of Baltimore County, as his guardian in 1806.

DORSEY, HENRY (son of Mathew Dorsey), no age given in 1808, was indentured with the consent of his father to David Malsby in 1808 to learn to be a blacksmith.

DORSEY, JOHN (son of Josias Dorsey), age 11 on June 1, 1820, was indentured to William Stump in 1821 to learn to be a farmer.

DORSEY, JOSIAS, father of Gabriel Dorsey and John Dorsey in 1821 indentures.

DORSEY, JUPITER (Negro orphan), age 16 on May 3, 1829, was indentured to Robert Cesky [?] in 1829 to learn to be a blacksmith.

DORSEY, MATHEW, father of Henry Dorsey in 1808 indenture.

DOUGHERTY, JOHN, master of Aquila Ayres (alias Davison) in 1807[?] indenture.

DOUGLASS, JOHN AND MARGARET, masters of Harriott Collins in 1804 indenture.

DOUGLASS, JOHN, master of John Collins (son of Ann Collins) in 1804 indenture.

DOVE, WILLIAM G., master of James Henry Dixon in 1830 indenture.

DREW, AQUILA, age 13 in June, 1803. Court appointed John Cole and Priscilla Cole as his guardians in 1803.

DREW, BENNET, age 12 in June, 1803. Court appointed John Cole and Priscilla Cole as his guardians in 1803.

DREW, FRANCES PRISCILLA, age 7 in April, 1821. Court appointed
Samuel Sutton and Martha, his wife, as her guardians in 1821.

DUBERRY, BENJAMIN, master of Richard McMurray (son of Margaret
McMurray) in 1802 indenture.

DUBERRY, BENJAMIN, master of Samuel Scarborough in 1801
indenture.

DUFF, JOHN, guardian of William Duff (orphan) in 1824.

DUFF, WILLIAM, age 17 on December 10, 1824, "his parents are
dead," was indentured to John Duff in 1824 to learn to be a
shoemaker.

DULANEY, JOSHUA, guardian of Polly and Martha Kimberly in 1808.

DULEY, AQUILA (orphan), age 17 on April 14, 1812, was indentured
to James S. McComas in 1812 to learn to be a carpenter.

DUNKEN, JOHN, master of John Kimble in 1813 indenture.

DURHAM, AMELIA (daughter of Elijah[?] Durham), age 8 in May,
1805. Court appointed John Denbow as her guardian in 1805.

DURHAM, ELIJAH[?], father of Amelia and Mahalah Durham in 1805.

DURHAM, MAHALAH (daughter of Elijah[?] Durham), age 10 in
November, 1805. Court appointed John Denbow as her guardian in
1805.

DUTTON, JOHN (son of Robert Dutton), age 18 on November 9, 1804.
Court appointed Aquila Norris as his guardian in 1805.

DUTTON, ROBERT, father of John Dutton in 1805 indenture.

EATON, JOHN H., master of Henry Martin (Negro) in 1827 indenture.

ECOFF, SAMUEL, master of Loisa [sic] Lytle in 1828 indenture.

EDGES, WILLIAM, age 14 on September 12, 1803. Court appointed
Andrew McAdow as his guardian in 1804.

EDWARD (Negro), age 7 on January 16, 1823, formerly bound to
Joshua Guyton, Sr., was now indentured to Josiah Guyton in
1823 to learn to be a farmer.

ELIZA (Negro, illegitimate), "age about 8 around December, 1828,"
was indentured to Richard Farmer in 1828 to learn to do
housework.

ELIZA (Negro), age 10 in July, 1815, was indentured to Mrs. Mary
Sears, of Havre de Grace, Maryland, in 1815.

ELIZOR (Negro), age 5 on December 4, 1813, was indentured with
the consent of her mother (not named) to Loyd Lee in 1813 to
learn to do housework.

ELLEN (Negro orphan), age 8 or 9 in 1812, was indentured to John
Harlen to learn to do housework.

ELLIOTT, ELIZABETH, "a poor girl," age 7 on March 22, 1829, was
indentured to John F. Wheeler in 1829 to learn to be a
housekeeper.

ELLIS, ELIZABETH, age 14 on March 16, 1817. Court appointed
Jamima Ellis as her natural guardian in 1817.

ELLIS, JAMIMA, natural guardian of Elizabeth Ellis, Samuel Ellis,
Nancy Ellis, Lesley Ellis, William Ellis, Marshal Ellis, and
Permelia Ellis in 1817.

ELLIS, JOHN JR., master of Charles Bradford (Negro) in 1801
indenture.

ELLIS, JOHN SR., master of Bill Bradford (Negro) in 1801
indenture.

ELLIS, LESLEY, age 8 on October 14, 1816. Court appointed Jamima
Ellis as his natural guardian in 1817.

ELLIS, MARSHAL, age 5 on April 29. 1817. Court appointed Jamima

Ellis as his natural guardian in 1817.

ELLIS, NANCY, age 10 on November 16, 1816. Court appointed Jamima Ellis as her natural guardian in 1817.

ELLIS, PERMELIA, age 2 on November 16, 1816. Court appointed Jamima Ellis as her natural guardian in 1817.

ELLIS, SAMUEL, age 12 on October 16, 1816. Court appointed Jamima Ellis as his natural guardian in 1817.

ELLIS, WILLIAM, age 6 on July 28, 1816. Court appointed Jamima Ellis as his natural guardian in 1817.

ELY, DAVID, age 19 on November 23, 1814. Court appointed Hannah Ely as his guardian in 1815.

ELY, HANNAH, guardian of David Ely in 1815.

EMANUEL (Negro son of Negro Charles), age 7 in 1802, was indentured to John Montgomery, Esq., in 1802 to learn to read, write and cipher.

ENGLAND, GEORGE, master of James Mitchell in 1809 indenture.

EPHRAIM (Colored), age about 25, was freed by the will of Mary Loney on April 1, 1826.

EVANS, AMOS, master of John Townsley in 1802 indenture.

EVANS, EVAN, master of Grafton Robinson Norrington in 1804 indenture.

EVATT, ELIZABETH (daughter of Richard Evatt), age 8 on May 1, 1809, was indentured to John Scarborough in 1809 to learn to do housework.

EVATT, JANE (daughter of Richard Evatt), age 10 on March 13, 1809, was indentured to James Howlett in 1809 to learn to do housework.

EVATT, RICHARD, father of Jane Evatt and Elizabeth Evatt in 1809 indentures.

EVELINA (Negro, illegitimate), age 5 on September 5, 1814, was indentured with the consent of her mother (not named) to Rachel Pearson in 1815 to learn to do housework.

EVEREST, SAMUEL, master of George Kimble in 1808 indenture.

EVERETT, WILLIAM, age 16 on January 1, 1806, was indentured with the consent of his mother (not named) to Richard Ashton in 1806 to learn to be a blacksmith.

EVERIST, BENJAMIN, guardian of John Whitaker, Emmale Whitaker, and Everist Whitaker in 1811.

EVERIST, CLARE, guardian of Francis Standish Everist, Mary Ann Everist, John Swann Everist, and Clarissa Everist in 1808.

EVERIST, CLARISSA, age 2 in February, 1808. Court appointed Clare Everist as her guardian in 1808.

EVERIST, FRANCIS STANDISH, age 14 on August 1, 1810, was indentured to James S. McComas in 1811 to learn to be a house carpenter.

EVERIST, FRANCIS STANDISH, age 11 in August, 1807. Court appointed Clare Everist as his guardian in 1808.

EVERIST, JOHN SWANN, age 4 in October, 1807. Court appointed Clare Everist as his guardian in 1808.

EVERIST, MARY ANN, age 9 in September, 1807. Court appointed Clare Everist as her guardian in 1808.

EVERITT, BENJAMIN, manumitted Negro Jack (son of Negro Mary) in 1805.

EWIN, JAMES, no age given on December 27, 1825, was indentured in 1826 with the consent of his parents (not named) to Timothy

Keen until May 24, 1829, to learn to be a blacksmith.

FAGG, BENJAMIN (brother of Robert Alman Fagg), age 8 on June 6, 1806, "their father abandoned them and their mother is not in this county," was indentured to Joshua Husbands in 1807 to learn to be a tanner.

FAGG, JOHN, age 12 in February, 1809, was indentured to Joshua Husbands in 1809 to learn to be a tanner.

FAGG, ROBERT ALMAN (brother of Benjamin Fagg), age 13 on April 9, 1806, "their father abandoned them and their mother is not in this county," was indentured to Joshua Husbands in 1807 to learn to be a tanner.

FANNY (Mulatto), age 7 on August 15, 1815, was indentured to Shadrack Streett in 1815 to learn to do housework.

FANNY (Negro daughter of Priss), age 11 in 1804, was indentured to John Ashton in 1804 to learn to do housework.

FANNY (Negro), age 15 months in August, 1811, was indentured with the consent of her mother (not named) to William Price and wife.

FANNY (Negro), age 4 on July 4, 1820, "now a pensioner" [sic], was indentured to Robert Martin in 1821 to learn to do housework.

FANNY (Negro), mother of Negro Isaac in 1828 indenture.

FANNY (Negro), mother of Negro Rachel in 1803 indenture.

FANNY (Negro), mother of Negro Isabella in 1807 indenture.

FARMER, RICHARD, master of Negro Isiah in 1826 indenture.

FARMER, RICHARD, master of Negro Eliza, Benedict Carr (Negro), and Benjamin Forwood (Negro) in 1828 indentures.

FELL, ELIJAH, master of Samuel Whiteford in 1804 indenture.

FERGUSON, JOHN, master of Joseph Fry in 1829 indenture.

FICKE, HERMAN (of Baltimore City), guardian of James Ficke in 1812.

FICKE, JAMES, age 9 on June 2, 1812. Court appointed Herman Ficke, of Baltimore City, as his guardian in 1812.

FICKIE, ANN, age 8 on March 2, 1815. Court appointed John Cain as her guardian in 1815.

FICKIE, JAMES, age 12 on June 2, 1815. Court appointed John Cain as his guardian in 1815.

FIE, NOBLE, age 14 on September 23, 1815. Court appointed John Cannon as his guardian in 1816.

FINNEY, WILLIAM, master of Sam Covey (Negro son of Judith Covey) in 1813 indenture.

FISHER, JAMES (son of Thomas Fisher), master of Elizabeth Clark in 1823 indenture.

FISHER, JOHN, age 10 years and 8 months in February, 1801, was indentured with the consent of his mother (not named) to James Cooper in 1801 to learn to be a cooper.

FISHER, MARGARET (orphan), age 11 on July 2, 1818, was indentured to Rutha Sheridine in 1818 to learn to do housework.

FISHER, THOMAS, father of James Fisher in 1823 indenture.

FITZGERALD, SIMON, master of William West (son of William West) in 1804 indenture.

FLAHERTY, HANNAH (orphan), age 11 on October 14, 1804, was indentured to Zenas Hughs to learn to do housework.

FLAHERTY, JOHN (orphan), age 14 on June 1, 1805, was indentured to Zenas Hughs in 1805 to learn to be a farmer.

FOARD, JAMES H., master of James Price in 1817 indenture.

FOARD, SOLOMON (orphan), age 15 on May 1, 1810, was indentured to David Maulsby in 1811 to learn to be a blacksmith.

FORD, DOROTHY, guardian of Samuel Hudson, James Hudson, Martha Hudson, and Sally Hudson in 1807.

FORD, JAMES, age 19 on July 19, 1818. Court appointed Martha Ford as his guardian in 1818.

FORD, MADISON (orphan), age 14 in June 21, 1827, was indentured to John Bevard in 1827 to learn to be a cooper.

FORD, MARTHA, guardian of James Ford and Mary Ford in 1818.

FORD, MARY, age 9 on January 24, 1818. Court appointed Martha Ford as her guardian in 1818.

FOREMAN, CHARLES, master of John Williams, Jr. in 1808 indenture.

FORWOOD, BENJAMIN (Negro), age 13 on May 3, 1828, was indentured to Richard Farmer in 1828 to learn to be a farmer.

FORWOOD, ELIZABETH, mother of John Forwood in 1805 indenture.

FORWOOD, JOHN (son of Elizabeth Forwood), age 16 on July 7, 1805, was indentured to George Smith in 1805 to learn to be a blacksmith.

FORWOOD, JOHN, guardian of William Loney Forwood in 1817.

FORWOOD, JOHN, guardian of John Brook, James Brook, and Sarah Brook in 1815.

FORWOOD, JOHN, guardian of John Johnson, William Parker Johnson, and Ann Elizabeth Johnson in 1813.

FORWOOD, JOHN, master of Nicholas Hooper in 1812 indenture.

FORWOOD, JONATHAN (orphan), age 16 on June 20, 1808, was indentured to Joshua Husbands in 1809 to learn to be a tanner.

FORWOOD, REUBEN, no age given in 1814, was indentured with the consent of his parents (not named) to Robert Barclay in 1814 to learn to be a cabinet maker.

FORWOOD, THOMAS P., age 6 on February 20, 1817. Court appointed Dr. Joseph Brownley as his guardian in 1817.

FORWOOD, WILLIAM LONEY, age 12 on February 10, 1817. Court appointed John Forwood as his guardian in 1817.

FOSTER, FREDERIC LEVI (son of John Foster), age 16 on May 26, 1806, was indentured to Ely Lucans in 1806 to learn to be a hatter.

FOSTER, JOHN, father of Frederic Levi Foster in 1806 indenture.

FOSTER, RACHEL, master of Sarah Harris in 1817 indenture.

FOX, EMANUEL (Colored), age 9 on September 1, 1828, was indentured with the consent of his mother (not named) to Henry O'Neal in 1828 to learn to be a farmer.

FOY, HENRY, master of Clark Hollis (son of Clark Hollis) in 1821 indenture.

FRANCES (Negro daughter of Negro Hetty), age 3 in September or October, 1809, was indentured with the consent of her mother to John Rouse in 1810 to do housework.

FRANCES (Negro), age about 1 year in 1825, and her mother Charlotte (Colored), age about 37, were freed by the will of Priscilla E. Bryarly on March 9, 1825.

FREEBORN (Negro), age 2 on September 1, 1802, was indentured with the consent of his mother (not named) to Barnet McComas in 1803 to learn to be a farmer.

FREEBORN (Negro), age 3 on January 1, 1802, was indentured with the consent of his mother (not named) to John Allen in 1802 to learn to be a farmer.

FRY, JOSEPH (orphan), age 19 on March 1, 1829, was indentured to John Ferguson in 1829 to learn to be a boot and shoemaker.

FULLARD, HENRY, master of George Patrick (son of Ruth Patrick) in 1804 indenture.

FULLERTON, JAMES, master of William Cotrall in 1801 and Ephraim Cottrall in 1804 indentures.

FULTON, ELIZABETH, guardian of Stephen J. Hanna in 1827.

FULTON, JAMES, master of Mary Spencer in 1815 indenture.

FULTON, JOSHUA, master of James M. Wheeler in 1821 indenture.

FURZE [TURZE?], SIMON (of Baltimore County), master of John Smith in 1815 indenture.

GABRIEL (Negro), age 4 on April 20, 1811, was indentured with the consent of his mother (not named) to John Monks in 1811 to learn to be a farmer.

GALLION, ALEXANDER, age 4 on January 28, 1816. Court appointed Alexander Gallion as his guardian in 1816.

GALLION, ALEXANDER, guardian of Elizabeth Gallion, Sarah Gallion, Ann Gallion, Joseph Gallion, Mary Gallion, Richard Gallion, and Alexander Gallion in 1816.

GALLION, ANN, age 12 in February, 1815. Court appointed Alexander Gallion as her guardian in 1816.

GALLION, ELIZA, age 14 on September 10, 1811. Court appointed Levi and Philazanna Howard as her guardian in 1812.

GALLION, ELIZABETH, age 15 in October, 1815. Court appointed Alexander Gallion as her guardian in 1816.

GALLION, HANNAH, age 13 in February, 1818. Court appointed Rhesa Norris as her guardian in 1818.

GALLION, HENRIETTA, age 7 on October 20, 1811. Court appointed Levi and Philazanna Howard as her guardian in 1812.

GALLION, JOHN (orphan), age 17 on February 17, 1816, was indentured to James Cochran in 1816 to learn to be a wheelwright.

GALLION, JOHN, age 20 in February, 1818. Court appointed Rhesa Norris as his guardian in 1818.

GALLION, JOHN PRESBURY, age 13 on February 13, 1812. Court appointed Levi and Philazanna Howard as his guardian in 1812.

GALLION, JOSEPH, age 10 on December 23, 1815. Court appointed Alexander Gallion as his guardian in 1816.

GALLION, MARY, age 8 in November, 1815. Court appointed Alexander Gallion as her guardian in 1816.

GALLION, RICHARD, age 6 on January 27, 1816. Court appointed Alexander Gallion as his guardian in 1816.

GALLION, SARAH, age 12 on August 22, 1815. Court appointed Alexander Gallion as her guardian in 1816.

GALLION, WILLIAM, age 16 in February, 1818. Court appointed Rhesa Norris as his guardian in 1818.

GALLION, WILLIAM BARREN FRANK, age 10 on May 6, 1812. Court appointed Levi and Philazanna Howard as his guardian in 1812.

GARRETT, ISAAC, age 17 on April 4, 1814, was indentured to Elijah Waskey in 1814 to learn to be a shoemaker.

GARRETT, RICHARD, age 12 on September 13, 1813, was indentured to Robert McComas in 1814 to learn to be a cabinet maker.

GARRETT, SAMUEL (Negro), age about 11 on March 1, 1822, "no parents in this county," was indentured to Edward Norris in

1822 to learn to be a farmer.

GARRETT, SAMUEL (orphan), age 9 in March, 1817, was indentured to Thomas Ayres in 1817 to learn to be a farmer.

GARRETTSON, AQUILA, age 17 on March 3, 1810. Court appointed Martha Garrettson as his guardian in 1810.

GARRETTSON, BENNETT, age 18 in June, 1809. Court appointed Martha Garrettson as his guardian in 1810.

GARRETTSON, GARRETT, age 14 on November 9, 1809. Court appointed James Garrettson as his guardian in 1810.

GARRETTSON, JAMES, by his 1805 will, freed Spencer Richardson (Negro) in January, 1828.

GARRETTSON, JAMES, guardian of Garrett Garrettson and Nimrod Garrettson in 1810.

GARRETTSON, MARTHA ELIZA, age 12 on October 9, 1809. Court appointed Martha Garrettson as her guardian in 1810.

GARRETTSON, MARTHA, guardian of Bennett Garrettson, Aquila Garrettson, and Martha Eliza Garrettson in 1810.

GARRETTSON, NIMROD, age 9 on November 9, 1809. Court appointed James Garrettson as his guardian in 1810.

GARRETTSON, SAMUEL JEFFERSON, age 17 on October 4, 1818, was indentured to Asa Burnett in 1818 to learn to be a blacksmith.

GARRISON, ANN, guardian of Samuel Garrison, James Garrison, Philip Garrison, and John Garrison in 1815.

GARRISON, JAMES, age 11 on July 10, 1815. Court appointed Ann Garrison as his guardian in 1815.

GARRISON, JANE AND THOMAS, guardians of Mary Warner in 1818.

GARRISON, JOHN, age 5 on January 12, 1815. Court appointed Ann Garrison as his guardian in 1815.

GARRISON, PHILIP, age 8 on December 4, 1814. Court appointed Ann Garrison as his guardian in 1815.

GARRISON, SAMUEL, age 14 on October 4, 1815. Court appointed Ann Garrison as his guardian in 1815.

GARRISON, THOMAS AND JANE, guardians of Mary Warner in 1818.

GEORGE (Negro orphan), age 14 in 1821, was indentured to Richard Qullum[?] in 1821 to learn to be a farmer.

GEORGE (Negro), age 3 on March 1, 1829, was indentured with the consent of his mother (not named) to Dr. Wakeman B. Hopkins in 1829 [no trade or craft was listed in the record].

GEORGE (Negro), age 8 on January 1, 1808, "destitute of support," was indentured to Israel D. Maulsby in 1809 to learn to be a house servant.

GERRARD (Negro, illegitimate), age 9 on December 10, 1827, was indentured to John Orrick Bagley in 1828 to learn to be a farmer.

GIBBS, JOHN (Negro orphan), age 2 on December 25, 1811, was indentured to Charles Gwinn (Negro) in 1812.

GIBERSON, HANNAH, mother of Hetty Giberson in 1802 indenture.

GIBERSON, HETTY (daughter of Hannah Giberson), no age given in 1802, was indentured to John Rouse and wife in 1802 to learn to do housework.

GIBSON, ANN MARIA, age 3 on June 24, 1818, was indentured with the consent of her mother, Hannah Gibson, to Samuel G. Parker in 1819.

GIBSON, BENJAMIN, master of Harry Bond (Negro) in 1820 indenture.

GIBSON, BENJAMIN, master of Carvil Moore in 1819 indenture.

GIBSON, HANNAH, mother of Ann Maria Gibson in 1819.

GIBSON, JAMES FRANKLIN (son of John Gibson, of Baltimore County), born February 8, 1817, was indentured to Elisha Bull, of Harford County, in 1827 to learn to be a miller in a grist mill.

GIBSON, JOHN, father of James Franklin Gibson in 1827 indenture.

GIBSON, JOHN, master of Eliza Cole (orphan) in 1815 indenture.

GILBERT, ABNER, master of Joseph Price (son of Robert Price) in 1808 indenture.

GILBERT, AMOS, master of George Grey and James Grey in 1813 indentures.

GILBERT, AMOS, master of William Henry Donaho in 1807 indenture.

GILBERT, AMOS, master of John Gray in 1809 indenture.

GILBERT, ANN MARTHA, age 7 on October 4, 1808. Court appointed Richard Mitchell as her guardian in 1809.

GILBERT, ANN MARTHA, age 10 months on August 4, 1802. Court appointed her father, Parker Gilbert, Jr., as her guardian.

GILBERT, CHARLES (son of Michael Gilbert), guardian of Clemency Gilbert, Elizabeth Gilbert, and William Gilbert in 1804.

GILBERT, CLEMENCY, age 15 on October 5, 1804. Court appointed Charles Gilbert (son of Michael Gilbert) as her guardian in 1804.

GILBERT, ELIZABETH, age 11 in 1809, went to Court in March, 1809, to have a guardian appointed [but none was named in the record].

GILBERT, ELIZABETH, age 12 on December 12, 1803. Court appointed Charles Gilbert (son of Michael Gilbert) as her guardian in 1804.

GILBERT, ELIZABETH, guardian of William Jolley Gilbert in 1811.

GILBERT, GEORGE THOMAS, age 8 on February 28, 1805. Court appointed Parker Gilbert, Sr. as his guardian in 1805, and then appointed Parker Gilbert (son of Parker Gilbert) as his guardian, also in 1805.

GILBERT, HENRY RUFF, age 18 "last fall," went to Court in March, 1809, to have a guardian appointed [but none was named in the record].

GILBERT, JACOB, master of Jarrett Ayres (son of Amelia Ayres) in 1815 indenture.

GILBERT, MARTIN T., master of Negro Moses in 1808 indenture.

GILBERT, MARY SOPHIA HALL, age 10 in January, 1805. Court appointed Parker Gilbert, Sr. as her guardian in 1805, and then appointed Parker Gilbert (son of Parker Gilbert) as her guardian, also in 1805.

GILBERT, MICHAEL, father of Charles Gilbert in 1804 indenture.

GILBERT, PARKER (son of Parker Gilbert), guardian of Mary Sophia Hall Gilbert and George Thomas Gilbert in 1805.

GILBERT, PARKER JR., father and guardian of Ann Martha Gilbert in 1802.

GILBERT, PARKER JR., master of Isaac Stallions and Thomas H. Gray in 1801 indentures.

GILBERT, PARKER, master of Amos Barnes and John Andrews in 1808 indentures.

GILBERT, PARKER, master of Garrett Barnes in 1804 indenture.

GILBERT, PARKER, master of James Thompson Donaho in 1807 indenture.

GILBERT, PARKER SR., guardian of Mary Sophia Hall Gilbert and George Thomas Gilbert in 1805.

GILBERT, PHILIP, age 13 in November, 1808, went to Court in March, 1809, to have a guardian appointed [but none was named in record].

GILBERT, WILLIAM, age 10 on December 28, 1803. Court appointed Charles Gilbert (son of Michael Gilbert) as his guardian in 1804.

GILBERT, WILLIAM JOLLEY, age 3 on September 1, 1810. Court appointed Elizabeth Gilbert as his guardian in 1811.

GILES, JACOB W., master of "a very white Mulatto boy John" in 1809 indenture.

GILES, JAMES, age 18 on January 8, 1808, was indentured with the consent of his mother, Rebecca Giles, to John O'Danel in 1807 to learn to be a carpenter and joiner.

GILES, REBECCA, mother of James Giles in 1807 indenture.

GILMORE, JOHN, age 12 on March 8, 1811, was indentured with the consent of his mother (not named) to William Divers in 1811 to learn to be a cooper.

GILMORE, WILLIAM, age 13 in 1807, was indentured to Richard Webster in 1807 to learn to be a miller.

GLADDEN, HUGH (illegitimate child of Jane Ruth), age 15 or 16 in 1808, was indentured to William McJilton in 1808 to learn to be a shoemaker.

GLASGOW, DELIVERANCE H., age 15 on July 7, 1829. Court appointed James Pannell (administrator of Elizh[?] Glasgow) as her guardian in 1830.

GLASGOW, ELIZH [?], deceased parent of Deliverance H. Glasgow, James Glasgow, and George R. Glasgow in 1830 guardianship.

GLASGOW, GEORGE R., age 7 on May 13, 1829. Court appointed James Pannell (administrator of Elizh[?] Glasgow) as his guardian in 1830.

GLASGOW, JAMES, age 10 on February 11, 1829. Court appointed James Pannell (administrator of Elizh[?] Glasgow) as his guardian in 1830.

GLENN, NATHAN, master of Amos Harry in 1818 indenture.

GOLDSBOROUGH, HOWES, master of William Pinnion in 1815 indenture.

GORDEN, MARGARET (illegitimate child), age 8 on September 16, 1816, was indentured with the consent of her mother (not named) to Thomas Mills in 1817 to learn to do housework.

GORRELL, ABRAHAM, master of Asael Pritchard in 1813 indenture.

GOUGH, CHARITY, age 7 in October, 1811. Court appointed Josiah S. McComas as her guardian in 1811.

GOUGH, HARRY DORSEY, age 19 on August 9, 1810. Court appointed John Hanna as his guardian in 1810.

GOUGH, PRUDENCE, age 15 in August, 1809. Court appointed Corbin Lee Onion as her guardian in 1810.

GOUGH, SUSANNAH, age 12 in April, 1811. Court appointed Corbin L. Onion as her guardian in 1811.

GOVER, ANTHONY (Negro), age 4 "the second week in December," 1809, was indentured with the consent of his mother, Sarah Gover (a free Negro woman), to William Bell in 1809 to learn to be a farmer.

GOVER, SARAH (a free Negro woman), mother of Anthony Gover (Negro) in 1809 indenture.

GRACE (Negro), mother of Negro Susannah in 1809 indenture.

GRAFTON, JANE AND WILLIAM, guardians of Ann Perine in 1801.

GRAFTON, JOHN, no age given in 1826. Court appointed Sarah Grafton as his guardian on August 8, 1826.

GRAFTON, NATHAN, master of James Numbers in 1812 indenture.

GRAFTON, SAMUEL, master of Salem Hough in 1812 indenture.

GRAFTON, SARAH, guardian of John Grafton in 1826.

GRAFTON, WILLIAM AND JANE, guardians of Ann Perine in 1801.

GRANT, THOMAS (orphan), age 14 in 1803, was indentured to Jacob Michael in 1803 to learn to be a farmer.

GRAY, GEORGE, master of William Burns in 1827 indenture.

GRAY, JOHN, age 16 on February 17, 1809, "abandoned by his father" (not named), was indentured with the consent of his mother (not named) to Amos Gilbert in 1809 to learn to be a boot and shoemaker.

GRAY, JOHN, master of Bennet Shay (illegitimate child) in 1821 indenture.

GRAY, THOMAS H., no age given in 1801, was indentured with the consent of his father (not named) to Parker Gilbert, Jr. in 1801 to learn to be a taylor.

GREEN, BENJAMIN JR., guardian of Michael Wheeler, Frances Wheeler, and Charity Teresa Wheeler in 1802.

GREEN, BENJAMIN, master of Levi Hagerthy (orphan) in 1806 indenture.

GREEN, JOHN, age 14 on May 1, 1818, was indentured to William Taylor in 1818 to learn to be a blacksmith.

GREEN, JOSHUA, master of Lunnon Colman (Negro son of Negro David Colman) in 1803 indenture.

GREENFIELD, ELIZABETH, age 4 on September 24, 1805. Court appointed Jacob Michael and/or Jacob Greenfield as her guardian(s) in 1805 [both names are given in subsequent entries].

GREENFIELD, HENRY AUSTIN, age 7 on October 30, 1804. Court appointed Jacob Michael and/or Jacob Greenfield as his guardian(s) in 1805 [both names are given in subsequent entries].

GREENFIELD, JACOB, age 6 on September 7, 1805. Court appointed Jacob Michael and/or Jacob Greenfield as his guardian(s) in 1805 [both names are given in subsequent entries].

GREENFIELD, JAMES, master of George Turk in 1810 indenture.

GREENFIELD, JAMES, master of William Brown in 1809 indenture.

GREENFIELD, JOSEPH, age 11 on January 1, 1805. Court appointed Jacob Michael and/or Jacob Greenfield as his guardian(s) in 1805 [both names are given in subsequent entries].

GREENFIELD, MARTHA, age 10 on October 6, 1805. Court appointed Jacob Michael and/or Jacob Greenfield as her guardian(s) in 1805 [both names are given in subsequent entries].

GREENFIELD, MARY, age 13 on September 3, 1805. Court appointed Jacob Michael and/or Jacob Greenfield as her guardian(s) in 1805 [both names are given in subsequent entries].

GREENFIELD, MICHAEL, guardian of Mary Greenfield, Joseph Greenfield, Martha Greenfield, Henry Austin Greenfield, Jacob Greenfield, and Elizabeth Greenfield in 1805.

GREENLAND, NATHANIEL (orphan), age 17 on June 11, 1809, was indentured to Benjamin Harbert, Jr. in 1810 to learn to be a weaver.

GREME, ANGUS, age 7 in 1801. Court appointed Mary Frances Greme as his guardian in 1801.

GREME, CAROLINE, age 2 in 1801. Court appointed Mary Frances Greme as her guardian in 1801.

GREME, FRANCES, age 10 in 1801. Court appointed Mary Frances Greme as her guardian in 1801.

GREME, HARRIOT, age 5 in 1801. Court appointed Mary Frances Greme as her guardian in 1801.

GREME, LAURA, age 8 in 1801. Court appointed Mary Frances Greme as her guardian in 1801.

GREME, MARY FRANCES, guardian of Frances Greme, Laura Greme, Harriot Greme, Caroline Greme, and Angus Greme in 1801.

GREY, GEORGE, age 16 on December 15, 1812, was indentured to Amos Gilbert in 1813 to learn to be a boot and shoemaker.

GREY, JAMES, age 14 on March 14, 1813, was indentured to Amos Gilbert in 1813 to learn to be a boot and shoemaker.

GRIFFIN, JOHN (Negro), age 19 on March, 19, 1829, "parents dead," was indentured to Jonathan Warner in 1829 to learn to be a farmer.

GRIFFIN, STEPHEN, age 17 on January 2, 1807, was indentured to William Griffith in 1806 to learn to be a farmer.

GRIFFITH, EDWARD, guardian of Alexander Lawson in 1808.

GRIFFITH, ELIZABETH, mother and guardian of Lewis Griffith in 1806.

GRIFFITH, GEORGE, master of William Presbury in 1817 indenture.

GRIFFITH, JAMES (orphan), age 14 on August 11, 1824, was indentured to Stephen A. Price [Pierce?] in 1825 to learn to be a hatter.

GRIFFITH, LEWIS (son of Elizabeth Griffith), age 2 "last spring" in 1806. Court appointed Elizabeth Griffith as his guardian in 1806.

GRIFFITH, WILLIAM, master of Stephen Griffin in 1806 indenture.

GRUPY, FRANCIS, master of Samuel Whiteford (orphan) in 1810 indenture.

GUBBINS, DAVID (son of Grace Gubbins), age 19 on April 15, 1804, was indentured to Thomas Kelly in 1804 to learn to be a cooper.

GUBBINS, GRACE, mother of David Gubbins in 1804 indenture.

GUEST, JOB AND ELIZABETH, guardians of John Wesley Cole and William Thomas Cole in 1811.

GUNNION, HUGH (son of Hugh Gunnion), age 3 years and 2 1/2 months in July, 1803, was indentured to Lazarus Mahon in 1803 to learn arithmetic and bookkeeping.

GUYTON, HENRY D., age 1 in June, 1821. Court appointed Jane Guyton as his guardian in 1822.

GUYTON, JANE, guardian of Henry D. Guyton in 1822.

GUYTON, JOSHUA SR., master of Negro Edward prior to 1823.

GUYTON, JOSIAH, master of Negro Edward in 1823 indenture.

GUYTON, ROBERT (illegitimate child), age 16 on March 20, 1813, was indentured with the consent of his mother (not named) to John Kennedy in 1813 to learn to be a weaver.

GWINN, CHARLES (Negro), master of John Gibbs (Negro) in 1812 indenture.

HAGARS (Negro), father of Negro Harriet in 1811 indenture.

HAGERTHY, LEVI (destitute orphan), age 14 in 1806, was indentured to Benjamin Green in 1806 to learn to be a cooper.

HAGERTY, ADAM (orphan), age 13 on January 1, 1811, was indentured to James Hathhorn in 1811 to learn to be a shoemaker.

HALL, ANN (daughter of John Hall), age 14 in March, 1805. Court appointed Caleb Hall as her guardian in 1806.

HALL, ANN, age 14 in June, 1806. Court appointed Edward Pearce as her guardian in 1806.

HALL, CALEB, guardian of Ann Hall (daughter of John Hall) in 1806.

HALL, EDWARD, one of the guardians of William White Hall in 1805.

HALL, ELISHA, age 19 in March, 1806. Court appointed Edward Pearce as his guardian in 1806.

HALL, ISABELLA, mother of William White Hall in 1805 guardianship.

HALL, JOHN, father of Ann Hall in 1806 guardianship.

HALL, NATHAN, age 14 on December 1, 1803. Court appointed John Rumsey as his guardian in 1804.

HALL, SOPHIA, guardian of Thomas W. Hall in 1818.

HALL, THOMAS W., age 18 on May 17, 1818. Court appointed Sophia Hall as his guardian in 1818.

HALL, WALTER T., master of John Williams (son of Martha Williams) in 1804 indenture.

HALL, WILLIAM, age 18 in December, 1803. Court appointed John Rumsey as his guardian in 1804.

HALL, WILLIAM, one of the guardians of William White Hall in 1805.

HALL, WILLIAM WHITE (son of Isabella Hall), age 11 on January 26, 1805. Court appointed William Hall and Edward Hall as his guardians in 1805.

HAMBY, JAMES, father of William Hamby in 1822 indenture.

HAMBY, WILLIAM (son of James Hamby), age 17 on July 11, 1822, was indentured to William Chesney in 1822 to learn to be a blacksmith.

HAMILTON, EDWARD, age 13 on September 16, 1822, was indentured to Miflin Beaumont in 1822 to learn to be a millwright.

HAMILTON, SHARLOTA, sister and nearest living relative of orphan George Knight in 1821 guardianship.

HAMMOND, WILLIAM, age 13 on December 4, 1801, was indentured to Joshua Husbands in 1802 to learn to be a tanner and currier.

HAMPTON (Colored, brother of Hannah), age 4 years and 5 months as of September 14, 1825, was indentured with the consent of his grandparents (not named) to Aquila B. Massey in 1825 to learn to be a farmer.

HANNA, ALEXANDER, master of Negro Avarilla in 1808 indenture.

HANNA, JOHN, guardian of Harry Dorsey Gough in 1810.

HANNA, STEPHEN J., age 16 on February 22, 1826. Court appointed Elizabeth Fulton as his guardian on February 13, 1827.

HANNA, WILLIAM, master of Bill Preston (Negro) in 1814 indenture.

HANNAH (Colored, sister of Hampton), age 9 years and 10 days as of September 14, 1825, was indentured with the consent of her grandparents (not named) to Aquila B. Massey in 1825 to learn to be a servant.

HANSON, BENEDICT, guardian of John C. Mathews, Milkey L. Mathews, Mary Elizabeth Mathews, William L. Mathews, and Mary Frances

Mathews in 1810.

HANWAY, DAVID, master of John Towson (son of Charles Towson) in 1803 indenture.

HANWAY, DAVID, master of Jesse James in 1801 indenture.

HANWAY, JOHN, master of William Criswell and Nancy Nowrey in 1806 indentures.

HANWAY, THOMAS, master of James McComas Amoss in 1830 indenture.

HANWAY, WASHINGTON, master of Martin Richardson in 1822 indenture.

HANWAY, WASHINGTON, master of William Turner in 1820 indenture.

HARBERT, BENJAMIN JR., master of Nathaniel Greenland in 1810 indenture.

HARKINS, AARON, father of John Harkins in 1802 indenture.

HARKINS, JOHN (son of Aaron Harkins), no age given in 1802, was indentured with the consent of his father to John Rouse in 1802 to learn to be a winsor [sic] chair and spinning wheel maker.

HARLEN, JOHN, master of Negro Ellen (orphan) in 1812 indenture.

HARRID, MARTHA, master of Mary Ann Middleditch in 1813 indenture.

HARRIETT (Negro), age 7 on May 25, 1808, was indentured to David Tate in 1808.

HARRIOT (Mulatto orphan), age 10 in July, 1815, was indentured to Mrs. Mary Sears, of Havre de Grace, Maryland, in 1815.

HARRIOT (Negro, illegitimate child of Negro Hagars), age 9 in March, 1811, was indentured to Euclidus Scarborough in 1811 to learn to do housework.

HARRIOT (Negro, illegitimate), age 6 on November 19, 1818 [sic], was indentured to Samuel H. Bayely in 1824 to learn to do housework.

HARRIS, SARAH (illegitimate child), age 9 on January 15, 1817, was indentured with the consent of her mother (not named) to Rachel Foster in 1817 to learn to do housework.

HARRY (Negro orphan), age 9 on August 1, 1815, was indentured with the consent of his mother (not named) to James Amoss in 1816 to learn to be a farmer.

HARRY (Negro), age 4 on May 25, 1819, was indentured to Daniel Weeks in 1819 to learn to be a farmer.

HARRY (Negro), age 10 years and 6 months in December, 1814, was indentured to Thomas Shay in 1813 to learn to be a farmer.

HARRY, AMOS, age 7 on July 18, 1817, was indentured with the consent of his mother (not named) to Nathan Glenn in 1818 to learn to be a farmer.

HARRY, DANIEL, master of Isaac Way (orphan) in 1811 indenture.

HARRY, ELI, age 5 on December 15, 1817, was indentured with the consent of his mother (not named) to John Doran in 1818 to learn to be a farmer.

HARRY, JOHN, master of Caleb Hitchcock in 1813 indenture.

HARRY, MARY, master of Eloner Connell in 1811 indenture.

HARRYMAN, HEZEKIAH, master of Negro Sukey in 1808 indenture.

HARVEY, ELIZABETH, age 5 in August, 1811, was indentured with the consent of her mother, Susanna Harvey, to James and Catharine Watkins in 1811.

HARVEY, JOHN, master of Wiley Davis (orphan) in 1815 indenture.

HARVEY, SUSANNA, mother of Elizabeth Harvey in 1811 indenture.

HASKELL, THOMAS, age 10 years and 7 months on November 25, 182C,

was indentured with the consent of his mother (not named) to
John O'Neill in 1820 to learn to be a nail and spike maker.

HATHHORN, JAMES, master of Adam Hagerty (orphan) in 1811
indenture.

HAWKINS, AVARILLA, age 6 in July, 1818. Court appointed Mary
Hawkins as her guardian in 1818.

HAWKINS, ELIZABETH, age 10 on March 4, 1818. Court appointed Mary
Hawkins as her guardian in 1818.

HAWKINS, GEORGE, age 5 in December, 1818. Court appointed Mary
Hawkins as his guardian in 1818.

HAWKINS, HOSEA, age 15 on July 25, 1810. Court appointed George
Smith as his guardian in 1811.

HAWKINS, JOHN, master of Alexander Cooper (son of John Cooper) in
1808 indenture.

HAWKINS, MARY, guardian of Elizabeth Hawkins, Avarilla Hawkins
and George Hawkins in 1818.

HAWKINS, MATHEW, master of Elizabeth Allendoffer in 1815
indenture.

HAWKINS, RICHARD, age 17 on August 2, 1810. Court appointed
George Smith as his guardian in 1811, and he was then
indentured to John Tucker in 1811 to learn to be a carpenter.

HAYES, ARCHER, guardian of John Young, Robert Young, Sarah Young,
Archer Hays Young, Thomas Jefferson Young, and Alexander Young
in 1806.

HAYS, THOMAS A., master of Ned Talbott (Negro) in 1805 indenture.

HEAPS, ABRAHAM, master of Jeremiah Connelly (orphan) in 1820
indenture.

HEAPS, WILLIAM, master of George Singleton in 1820 indenture.

HEATON, JOHN, master of Richard Singleton in 1822 indenture.

HELLEN, ALEXANDER, guardian of John Hellen and Mary Ann Hellen in
1807.

HELLEN, JOHN, age 7 in April, 1807. Court appointed Alexander
Hellen as his guardian in 1807.

HELLEN, MARY ANN, age 5 in April, 1807. Court appointed Alexander
Hellen as her guardian in 1807.

HELLER, JOHN, age 15 on January 7, 1812, "abandoned by parents,"
was indentured to Thomas Brown in 1812 to learn to be a
farmer.

HENARY (Negro), age 10 years and 4 months on November 21, 1812,
was indentured with the consent of his mother (not named) to
William McMath in 1812 to learn to be a farmer.

HENDAN [HENDON?], JAMES, master of Henry Cook in 1823 indenture.

HENDERSON, ARCHABALD, master of John Walton (Negro) in 1830
indenture.

HENDERSON, ARCHIBALD, age 6[?] on August 27, 1816. Court
recognized Sarah Henderson as his natural guardian in 1817.

HENDERSON, SARAH, age 15 on August 3, 1816. Court recognized
Sarah Henderson as her natural guardian in 1817.

HENDERSON, SARAH, recognized by the Court as the natural guardian
of Thomas N. Henderson, Sarah Henderson and Archibald
Henderson in 1817.

HENDERSON, THOMAS N., age 18 on February 8, 1817. Court
recognized Sarah Henderson as his natural guardian in 1817.

HENRY (Negro), age 10 on December 27, 1824, was indentured by his
own consent to John Brown in 1825 to learn to be a farmer.

HENRY (Negro), age about 17 in 1823, valued at $250, and formerly owned by William Calwell, deceased, in October, 1823.

HENRY (Negro), no age given in 1822, formerly indentured to Thomas Shay on December 12, 1814, "but he [Shay] lately died, leaving no widow," now indentured with the consent of his mother (not named) to Jason Moore in 1822 to learn to be a farmer.

HENRY, CHARLES, age 14 on February 1, 1815, was indentured with the consent of his mother (not named) to William Kirk in 1815 to learn to be a wheelwright.

HENRY, JAMES (Negro), age 3 on December 27, 1816, was indentured with the consent of his mother (not named) to Alexander McComas in 1816 to learn to be a farmer.

HENRY, JOHN, age 11 on May 15, 1808, was indentured with the consent of his mother (not named) to Ephraim Swart in 1809 to learn to be a wheelwright.

HERBERT, JANE, master of Sarah Coine (Negro) in 1829 indenture.

HERREN, CHARLES (illegitimate child), age 10 on March 9, 1808, was indentured with the consent of his mother (not named) to John Pogue in 1808 to learn to be a farmer.

HETTY (Negro), mother of Negro Frances (orphan) in 1810 indenture.

HILL, AARON, guardian of Copeland Timmons in 1809.

HILL, ANN MARIA GREEN, age 14 on December 16, 1816. Court recognized Martha Hudson as her natural guardian in 1817.

HILL, BETTY (Negro), mother of John "Jack" Hill (Negro) and Suckey Hill (Negro) in 1802 indenture.

HILL, HANNAH WRIGHT, age 12 on October 6, 1816. Court recognized Martha Hudson as her natural guardian in 1817.

HILL, HENRY (Mulatto), age 8 in September, 1810, was indentured to John Watters in 1810 to learn to be a farmer.

HILL, HENRY (orphan), age 17 years and 3 months as of June 24, 1825, "leaving no father or as known mother living," was indentured to Mortimore Cunningham in 1825 to learn to be a house carpenter.

HILL, JOHN "JACK" (Negro son of Betty Hill, Negro), age 7 in 1802, was indentured to ---- Butler in 1802 to learn to be a farmer.

HILL, JOHN G., age 14 on January 15, 1816. Court appointed William Allen as his guardian in 1816.

HILL, MILCHA BROWNING, age 9 on March 5, 1816. Court recognized Martha Hudson as her natural guardian in 1817.

HILL, MOSES, age 16 on November 4, 1816, was indentured with the consent of his mother (not named) to Ephraim Swart in 1817 to learn to be a cart and wagon maker.

HILL, REBECCA, age 7 on April 11, 1816. Court recognized Martha Hudson as her natural guardian in 1817.

HILL, SUCKEY (Negro), daughter of Betty Hill, Negro), age 4 in 1802, was indentured to ---- Butler in 1802 to learn to read and do housework.

HILTON, ABRAHAM (Negro), son of David Hilton, age 9 in January, 1804, was indentured to Ralph Sackett Lee in 1804 to learn to be a miller.

HILTON, DAVID (Negro), father of Abraham Hilton in 1804 indenture.

HIPKINS, CHARLES, guardian of Elizabeth Debrular in 1802.
HIPKINS, THOMAS, age about 14 on March 19, 1827. Court appointed
  Thomas Dorney as his guardian in 1828 [Died a minor?].
HITCHCOCK, AMELINE, age 14 in 1809. Court appointed Israel D.
  Maulsby as her guardian in 1809.
HITCHCOCK, BELINDA (illegitimate child), age 9 on January 8,
  1827, was indentured with the consent of her mother (not
  named) to Robert McClung in 1827 to learn to do housework.
HITCHCOCK, BILLENDER (illegitimate child), age 9 on January 8,
  1827, was indentured with the consent of her mother (not
  named) to Robert McClung in 1828 to learn to do housework.
HITCHCOCK, CALEB, no age given in March, 1813, was indentured
  with the consent of his father (not named) to John Harry in
  1813 [name of trade or craft not given].
HITCHCOCK, CHARITY, mother of Aquila Hitchcock in 1806 indenture.
HITCHCOCK, DENNIS, age 2 in 1809. Court appointed Israel D.
  Maulsby as his guardian in 1809.
HITCHCOCK, DENNIS, age 11 in October, 1818. Court appointed
  Thomas Ayres, Sr. as his guardian in 1819.
HITCHCOCK, ELIZABETH (illegitimate), age 14 years and 7 months in
  February, 1829, was indentured to John Kennedy in 1829 to
  learn to do housewifery.
HITCHCOCK, ELIZABETH, age 8 in 1809. Court appointed Israel D.
  Maulsby as her guardian in 1809.
HITCHCOCK, ESTHER, mother of Luther Hitchcock in 1815 indenture.
HITCHCOCK, JARRETT, age 5 in 1809. Court appointed Israel D.
  Maulsby as his guardian in 1809.
HITCHCOCK, JARRETT, age 14 in October, 1818. Court appointed
  Thomas Ayres, Sr. as his guardian in 1819.
HITCHCOCK, JASON, age 12 in 1809. Court appointed Israel D.
  Daulsby as his guardian in 1809.
HITCHCOCK, LUTHER (son of Esther Hitchcock), age 16 on December
  4, 1815, was indentured to William Mills in 1815 to learn to
  be a taylor.
HITCHCOCK, LUTHER, age 7 in 1809. Court appointed Israel D.
  Maulsby as his guardian in 1809.
HITCHCOCK, LUTHER, age 16 in October, 1818. Court appointed
  Thomas Ayres, Sr. as his guardian in 1819.
HOALE, HUSBAND, master of Samuel Cotts in 1807 indenture.
HOLLAND, FRANCIS W., father of John Francis Augustus Holland in
  1814 indenture.
HOLLAND, JOHN FRANCIS AUGUSTUS (son of Francis W. Holland), no
  age given in 1814, was indentured to John Moores in December,
  1814, to learn to be a tanner and currier.
HOLLINGSWORTH, NATHANIEL, master of Alice Johnson (orphan) in
  1814 indenture.
HOLLIS, AMOS, father of Chauncey Hollis in 1817 indenture.
HOLLIS, CHAUNCEY (son of Amos Hollis), age 17 on March 31, 1817,
  was indentured to Daniel Bradford and Robert Bradford in 1817
  to learn to be a cabinet maker.
HOLLIS, CLARK (son of Clark Hollis), age 17 on December 1, 1820,
  was indentured to Henry Foy in 1821 to learn to be a
  shoemaker.
HOLLIS, CLARK, father of Clark Hollis in 1821 indenture.
HOLLIS, CLARK, guardian of Jane Lytle in 1815.

HOOPER, NICHOLAS, age 19 on June 12, 1814, was indentured with
the consent of his father (not named) to Timothy Keen in 1813
to learn to be a blacksmith.

HOOPER, NICHOLAS, no age given in April, 1812, was indentured
with the consent of his father (not named) to John Forwood to
learn to be a blacksmith.

HOOPMAN, ISAAC, master of George Knight in 1821 indenture.

HOPE, EZRA, natural guardian of Ruth Hope, Hannah Hope, Thomas
Hope, and Nicholas H. Hope in 1816.

HOPE, HANNAH, age 12 in June, 1815. Court recognized Ezra Hope as
her natural guardian in 1816.

HOPE, NICHOLAS H., age 5 in June, 1815. Court recognized Ezra
Hope as his natural guardian in 1816.

HOPE, RUTH, age 14 on December 19, 1815. Court recognized Ezra
Hope as her natural guardian in 1816.

HOPE, THOMAS, age 9 in September, 1815. Court recognized Ezra
Hope as his natural guardian in 1816.

HOPKINS, EPHRAIM, guardian of Margaret Morgan in 1804.

HOPKINS, EPHRAIM, master of Negro John in 1820 indenture.

HOPKINS, ISAAC (Negro), father of Jacob Hopkins in 1802
indenture.

HOPKINS, JACOB (Negro son of Isaac Hopkins), no age given in
1802, was indentured to Robert Carr in 1802 to learn to be a
farmer.

HOPKINS, JOSEPH, father of Samuel Hopkins in 1816 indenture.

HOPKINS, SAMUEL (son of Joseph Hopkins), master of Negro Nancy in
1816 indenture.

HOPKINS, SAMUEL, master of Margarett Waters in 1817 indenture.

HOPKINS, WAKEMAN B. (Doctor), master of Negro George in 1829
indenture.

HOSEA (Negro, illegitimate child of Negro Nelley), age 9 months
on June 7, 1811, was indentured to James Howlet in 1811 to
learn to be a farmer.

HOUGH, SALEM, age 4 on October 27, 1811, was indentured with the
consent of his mother (not named) to Samuel Grafton in 1812 to
learn to be a farmer.

HOW, JAMES (orphan), age 13 in January, 1814, was indentured to
Isaac Perryman in 1814 to learn to be a farmer.

HOW, JOHN (son of William How), no age given in 1801, was
indentured to Isaac Cooper in 1801 to learn to be a cooper.

HOW, THOMAS (son of William How), age 17 on September 2, 1808,
was indentured to John Steele in 1809 to learn to be a
blacksmith.

HOW, WILLIAM (son of William How), no age given in 1801, was
indentured to Isaac Towson in 1801 to learn to be a cooper.

HOW, WILLIAM, father of Thomas How in 1809 indenture.

HOW, WILLIAM, father of John How and William How in 1801
indenture.

HOWARD, ANN M., age 9 on March 17, 1811. Court appointed James W.
Tolley as her guardian in 1811.

HOWARD, ELIZA M., age 11 on December 20, 1811. Court appointed
James W. Tolley as her guardian in 1811.

HOWARD, JAMES T., age 5 on January 16, 1811. Court appointed
James W. Tolley as his guardian in 1811.

HOWARD, JONATHAN (Colored), age 14 on September 10, 1824, was

indentured with the consent of his mother (not named) to
Howard Mason in 1824 to learn to be a farmer.

HOWARD, LEVI AND PHILAZANNA, guardians of Eliza Gallion, John
Presbury Gallion, William Barren Frank Gallion, and Henrietta
Gallion in 1812.

HOWARD, SUSAN, age 7 on March 18, 1811. Court appointed James W.
Tolley as her guardian in 1811.

HOWARD, THOMAS C.[G?], age 14 on December 2, 1811. Court
appointed George G. Presbury, of Baltimore City, as his
guardian in 1812.

HOWARD, THOMAS G., age 14 on December 20, 1811. Court appointed
James W. Tolley as his guardian in 1811.

HOWLET, JAMES, master of Negro Hosea (son of Negro Nelley) in
1811 indenture.

HOWLETT, JAMES, master of Jane Evatt (daughter of Richard Evatt)
in 1809 indenture.

HOWLETT, JOHN, master of Isaac Wilson in 1817 indenture.

HUDSON, JAMES, age 12 on April 9, 1807. Court appointed Dorothy
Ford as his guardian in 1807.

HUDSON, MARTHA, age 9 on May 9, 1806. Court appointed Dorothy
Ford as her guardian in 1807.

HUDSON, MARTHA, natural guardian of Ann Maria Green Hill, Hannah
Wright Hill, Milcha Browning Hill, and Rebecca Hill in 1817.

HUDSON, SALLY, age 7 in March, 1807. Court appointed Dorothy Ford
as her guardian in 1807.

HUDSON, SAMUEL, age 13 in April, 1806. Court appointed Dorothy
Ford as his guardian in 1807.

HUDSON, SAMUEL, age 16 on April 7, 1809, was indentured to Elihu
Allender in 1809 to learn to be a shoemaker.

HUFF, ABRAHAM, master of David West and William West in 1809
indenture.

HUFF, JACKSON, age 5 on February 11, 1819, was indentured to ----
[no name given in record] in 1819 to learn to be a miller.

HUGHES, ELIZA JANE (Colored, daughter of Ignatius Hughes, of
Baltimore County), age 4 in 1827, was indentured to Robert
Kirkwood, Sr., of Harford County, on July 15, 1827, to learn
to do housework.

HUGHES, IGNATIUS, father of Eliza Jane Hughes in 1827 indenture.

HUGHES, JOHN, master of William Cristy (Negro) in 1828 indenture.

HUGHES, SCOTT, master of Henry Knight in 1802 indenture.

HUGHES, WILLIAM, see "William Chesney (alias Cain or Hughes)."

HUGHS, ZENAS, master of John Flaherty and Hannah Flaherty in 1805
indentures.

HUNTER, WILLIAM JR., master of Robert Knight (son of Ann Knight)
in 1815 indenture.

HUNTER, WILLIAM, master of America Courtney in 1823 indenture.

HUSBAND, JOSHUA, master of Richard Wheeler in 1804 indenture.

HUSBAND, MYRTILLA (Negro), born May 15, 1811, daughter of Rachel
Husband (Negro), was indentured to Elizabeth Quarles in 1811
to learn to do housework.

HUSBAND, RACHEL (Negro), mother of Myrtilla Husband in 1811
indenture.

HUSBANDS, JOHN, master of Moses Kaufman in 1828 indenture.

HUSBANDS, JOSHUA, master of John Fagg and Jonathan Forwood in
1809 indentures.

HUSBANDS, JOSHUA, master of Robert Alman Fagg and Benjamin Fagg in 1807 indentures.

HUSBANDS, JOSHUA, master of Moses Kaufman in 1828 indenture.

HUSBANDS, JOSHUA, master of Henry Miller in 1801 indenture.

HUSBANDS, JOSHUA, master of John Young in 1805 indenture.

HUSBANDS, JOSHUA, master of William Hammond in 1802 indenture.

HUSBANDS, JOSHUA, master of Eli Lewis in 1804 indenture.

IRVIN, WILLIAM, guardian of John Wilson, James Wilson, and William Wilson in 1825.

ISAAC (Negro, son of Fanny), age 7 in November, 1827, was indentured to Ann Weeks in 1828 to learn to be a farmer.

ISAAC (Negro), age 8 in May, 1801, was indentured to David Lee in 1801 to learn to be a farmer.

ISAAC (Negro), age 4 in September, 1807, was indentured with the consent of his mother (not named) to Thomas Tredway in 1808 to learn to be a cooper.

ISABELLA (Negro), daughter of Negro Fanny, age 4 years and 1 month in December, 1807, was indentured to Henry Stump, Jr. in 1807 to learn to do housework.

ISIAH (Negro orphan), age 6 on January 1, 1826, was indentured to Richard Farmer in 1826 to learn to be a farmer.

JACK (Negro), age 6 on December 25, 1804, son of Negro Mary, was manumitted by Benjamin Everitt and indentured to Hugh Deaver in 1805 to learn to be a farmer.

JACKSON, DANIEL (orphan), age 16 on February 5, 1810, was indentured in 1810 to Upton Reed & Rees Davis, cutlers, to learn to be a spade and shovel maker.

JACKSON, JOHN, master of John Bond (orphan) in 1808 indenture.

JACOB (Negro, illegitimate), born on January 15, 1821, was indentured with the consent of his mother (not named) to John Dever on November 24, 1825, to learn to be a farmer.

JAMES (Negro, illegitimate), age 5 on December 25, 1804, was indentured to Charles Watters (Negro) in 1805 to learn to be a farmer.

JAMES (Negro orphan), age 14 on August 1, 1819, was indentured to James Amoss in 1819 to learn to be a farmer.

JAMES, ELIAKIM, deceased father of William James in 1808 indenture.

JAMES, JESSE, age 11 in 1801, was indentured to David Hanway in 1801 to learn to be a miller.

JAMES, WILLIAM (son of Eliakim James, deceased), age 9 on October 16, 1807, was indentured to Joshua Branson in 1808 to learn to be a farmer.

JANE (Negro), age 5 on November 1, 1818, was indentured to Jason Moore in 1819 to learn to do housework.

JANE (Negro), mother of free Negro Sarah in 1806 indenture.

JAY, JOHN, age 20 months in October, 1818. Court recognized Martha Jay as his natural guardian in 1818.

JAY, JOSEPH, master of Eleanor McClannon (orphan) in 1804 indenture.

JAY, MARTHA, natural guardian of John Jay in 1818.

JAY, MARY (Negro), age 7 on June 1, 1829, was indentured with the consent of her mother (not named) to Henry O'Neil in 1829 to learn to be a servant.

JAY, THOMAS, guardian of George Austin, Edward Austin, Colegate

Austin, and Esther Austin in 1817.

JAY, THOMAS, master of William Miller in 1801 indenture.

JEFFERIES, VINCENT (son of William Jefferies), age 17 on April 1, 1805, was indentured to John Davis in 1805 to learn to be a boot and shoemaker.

JEFFERIES, WILLIAM, father of Vincent Jefferies in 1805 indenture.

JEFFERSON (Negro), age about 15 in 1823, valued at $200, and formerly owned by William Calwell, deceased, in October, 1823.

JEFFERY, THOMAS, guardian of John Boyd Bell, James Lucky Bell, and Rebecca Cochran Bell in 1808.

JEFFERY, THOMAS, guardian of Harriott Bayless in 1802.

JEFFERY, THOMAS, guardian of James Bayless in 1803.

JEFFERY, VINCENT, master of William Curry (son of James Curry) in 1820 indenture.

JEFFREY, JOHN WESLEY, age 10 on October 29, 1829, was indentured with the consent of his mother (not named) to Abraham Spicer in 1829 to learn to be a stone mason.

JERVIS, BENJAMIN, master of James Perry (orphan) in 1806 indenture.

JEWETT, JOHN, master of Jacob Chew (son of Roger Chew) in 1810 indenture.

JEWETT, JOHN, master of Nat Preston (Negro son of Sam Preston, a free Negro) in 1811 indenture.

JOHN ("a very white Mulatto boy"), age 12 in 1809, was indentured to Jacob W. Giles in 1809 to learn to be a farmer.

JOHN (Negro, illegitimate), age 13 on July 15, 1822, was indentured with the consent of his mother (not named) to William Worthington in 1822 to learn to be a farmer.

JOHN (Negro, illegitimate), age 5 in March, 1817, was indentured with the consent of his mother (not named) to Samuel Lee Webster in 1817 to learn to be a farmer.

JOHN (Negro, illegitimate), age 7 on August 15, 1819, was indentured to Ephraim Hopkins in 1820 to learn to be a farmer.

JOHN (Negro orphan), age 15 in October, 1819, was indentured to Aquila Massey in 1820 to learn to be a farmer.

JOHN (Negro), age 5 on April 1, 1816, was indentured with the consent of his mother (not named) to John Dever in 1816 to learn to be a farmer.

JOHN (Negro), age 13 on September 27, 1825, was indentured with the consent of his mother (not named) to William Worthington in 1826 to learn to be a farmer.

JOHNES, HANNAH (Colored), age 6 in September, 1825, was indentured with the consent of her mother (not named) to Henry C. Neall in 1825 to learn to do housework.

JOHNS, FRANCIS, of Abingdon, Maryland, master of Daniel McCarty in 1823 indenture.

JOHNSON, ALICE (orphan), age 10 on February 3, 1814, was indentured to Nathaniel Hollingsworth in 1814 to learn to do housework.

JOHNSON, ANN ELIZABETH, no age given in 1813. Court appointed John Forwood as her guardian in 1813.

JOHNSON, BARNETT (son of Barnett Johnson), guardian of Richard Ward in 1802.

JOHNSON, CHANY [CHANCY?], (son of James Johnson, deceased), age 9 in October, 1820. Court appointed David Malsby as his guardian in 1821.

JOHNSON, DOROTHY, master of Cassandra Tayson (illegitimate child) and Mary Ann Tayson (orphan) in 1810 indentures.

JOHNSON, ELIZABETH, by her 1820 will, freed Martha Williams (Negro) in March, 1828.

JOHNSON, ELY (son of James Johnson, deceased), age 6 in September, 1821. Court appointed David Malsby as his guardian in 1821.

JOHNSON, GEORGE, age 15 on July 31, 1822, was indentured with the consent of his mother (not named) to William H. Pierce in 1822 to learn to be a hatter.

JOHNSON, HANNAH (daughter of James Johnson, deceased), age 11 in August, 1821. Court appointed David Malsby as her guardian in 1821.

JOHNSON, ISAAC (Negro), age about 12 in November, 1830, was indentured to Abraham Rutledge in 1830 to learn to be a farmer.

JOHNSON, JAMES, age 17 on April 10, 1822, was indentured with the consent of his mother (not named) to William H. Pierce in 1822 to learn to be a hatter.

JOHNSON, JAMES AND MARY, deceased parents of Milton Johnson and John Johnson in 1820 indentures.

JOHNSON, JAMES AND FANNY, parents of Stephen Johnson (Negro) and Nancy Johnson (Negro) in 1812 indenture.

JOHNSON, JAMES, deceased father of Milton Johnson, John Johnson, Thomas Johnson, Robert Johnson, Hannah Johnson, Chany [Chancy?] Johnson, Joseph Johnson, Sarah Johnson, Ely Johnson, Mary Ann Johnson, and Pheba Johnson in 1821 guardianships.

JOHNSON, JOHN (son of James and Mary Johnson, both deceased), age 12 in October, 1819, was indentured to James S. McComas in 1820 to learn to be a carpenter and joiner. Court appointed David Malsby as his guardian in 1821.

JOHNSON, JOHN, age 7 on November 7, 1812. Court appointed John Forwood as his guardian in 1813.

JOHNSON, JOHN, master of George Murray (Negro) in 1829 indenture.

JOHNSON, JOSEPH (son of James Johnson, deceased), age 9 in September, 1821. Court appointed David Malsby as his guardian in 1821.

JOHNSON, JOSIAH, master of Stephen Johnson and Nancy Johnson in 1812 indentures.

JOHNSON, JOSIAS (Colored), age 5 on November 25, 1823, was indentured with the consent of his mother (not named) to Samuel Wilson in 1824 to learn to be a farmer.

JOHNSON, LEVI ("a free black, illegitimate child"), age 7 on April 20, 1806, was indentured with the consent of his mother (not named) to Moses G. Smith in 1806 to learn to be a miller.

JOHNSON, MARY ANN (daughter of James Johnson, deceased), age 5 in February, 1821. Court appointed David Malsby as her guardian in 1821.

JOHNSON, MARY, stepmother of Thomas Johnson in 1815 indenture.

JOHNSON, MICHAEL, age 16 on May 18, 1813, was indentured with the consent of his mother (not named) to Jonathan Vanhorn in 1813 to learn to be a blacksmith.

JOHNSON, MILTON (son of James and Mary Johnson, both deceased), age 14 in February, 1820, was indentured to James S. McComas in 1820 to learn to be a carpenter and joiner. Court appointed David Malsby as his guardian in 1821.

JOHNSON, NANCY (Negro daughter of James and Fanny Johnson), age 4 on October 15, 1812, was indentured to Josiah Johnson in 1812.

JOHNSON, PHEBA (daughter of James Johnson, deceased), age 3 in May, 1821. Court appointed David Malsby as her guardian in 1821.

JOHNSON, ROBERT (Negro), now age 31, and by the will of William Morgan, is now free, December 15, 1826.

JOHNSON, ROBERT (orphan), age 18 on July 1, 1826, was indentured to Stephen A. Peerce in 1826 to learn to be a hatter.

JOHNSON, ROBERT (son of James Johnson, deceased), age 12 in July, 1821. Court appointed David Malsby as his guardian in 1821.

JOHNSON, SARAH (daughter of James Johnson, deceased), age 8 in March, 1821. Court appointed David Malsby as her guardian in 1821.

JOHNSON, STEPHEN (Negro son of James and Fanny Johnson), age 5 on October 15, 1812, was indentured to Josiah Johnson in 1812 to learn to be a farmer.

JOHNSON, THOMAS (son of James and Mary Johnson, both deceased), age 13 in October, 1820. Court appointed David Malsby as his guardian in 1821.

JOHNSON, THOMAS (stepson of Mary Johnson), age 14 on March 1, 1815, was indentured to James Keer [Kerr?] in 1815 to learn to be a spinning wheel maker.

JOHNSON, THOMAS, age 16 in October, 1823, was indentured to James S. McComas in 1823 to learn to be a carpenter.

JOHNSON, WILLIAM PARKER, age 3 on October 5, 1812. Court appointed John Forwood as his guardian in 1813.

JOHNSTON, HANNAH, mother of Thomas Waltham (an illegitimate child) in 1823 indenture.

JONES, ANN (daughter of Frances Jones), age 7 years and 4 months in March, 1803, was indentured to John Lane in 1803 to learn to do housework.

JONES, EZEKIEL (orphan), age 16 on January 1, 1804, was indentured to Morris Maulsby in 1804 to learn to be a blacksmith.

JONES, FRANCES, mother of Ann Jones in 1803 indenture.

JONES, GILBERT AND SALLY, masters of Negro Sabina in 1801 indenture.

JONES, RICHARD H., master of Aaron Morings (Negro) in 1805 indenture.

JONES, SALLY AND GILBERT, masters of Negro Sabina in 1801 indenture.

JONES, WILLIAM, age 17 years and 3 1/2 months in September, 1806, was indentured with the consent of his mother (not named) to Ephraim Swart in 1807 to learn to be a wagon maker.

JORDAN, GEORGE (orphan), age 9 on May 11, 1825, "having no parents in the county," was indentured to William Coale in 1825 [no trade or craft listed in record].

JORDAN, JOHN, guardian of William M. Jordan in 1827.

JORDAN, WILLIAM M., age 12 on November 5, 1826. Court appointed John Jordan as his guardian on January 16, 1827.

JORDON, JOHN, master of Hugh McGonegal (son of Daniel McGonegal) in 1811 indenture.

JOSIAS (Negro), age 11 on April 1, 1819, was indentured to James
S. McComas in 1819 to learn to do rough carpenter work.

JUDA (Negro), age about 8 in 1801, was indentured to James and
Neomah Michael in 1801 to learn to do housework.

JUDD, EDWARD, master of James Norrington (son of Sarah
Norrington) in 1821 indenture.

JUDD, JOHN, master of Elizabeth R. Criswell in 1828 indenture.

JUINS, WILLIAM, "an abandoned child," age 14 in May, 1821, was
indentured to Timothy Keen in 1821 to learn to be a
blacksmith.

JULIET (Negro orphan), age 7 in May, 1811, was indentured to
Alesanna Kell in 1811 to learn to do housework.

KAUFMAN, MOSES (orphan), age 8 on November 29, 1827, was
indentured to Joshua and John Husbands in 1828 to learn to be
a tanner.

KEAN, JOHN, guardian of Susan Thompson and John Thompson in 1821.

KEEN, TIMOTHY, master of William Juins in 1821 indenture.

KEEN, TIMOTHY, master of Nicholas Hooper in 1813 indenture.

KEEN, TIMOTHY, master of Stephen Dorney in 1806 indenture.

KEEN, TIMOTHY, master of James Ewin in 1826 indenture.

KELL, ALESANNA, master of Negro Juliet and Negro Moses in 1811
indentures.

KELLY, THOMAS, master of Daniel Gubbins (son of Grace Gubbins)
and Jacob Burkins in 1804 indentures.

KENLEY, LEMUEL, guardian of Nathaniel Bayless in 1803.

KENLEY, LEWIS (Negro), age 4 years and 10 months in July, 1822,
was indentured with the consent of his mother (not named) to
William Wallis in 1822 to learn to be a farmer.

KENLEY, RICHARD (Negro), age 8 in 1822, was indentured with the
consent of his mother (not named) to William Wallis in 1822 to
learn to be a farmer.

KENNEDY, JAMES, master of Negro Corbin in 1815 indenture.

KENNEDY, JOHN, master of Robert Guyton in 1813 indenture.

KENNEDY, JOHN, master of Elizabeth Hitchcock in 1829 indenture.

KENTLEMYRES, ALEXANDER, age 6 in 1810. Court appointed Margaret
Kentlemyers as his guardian in 1810.

KENTLEMYRES, HARRIOT, age 8 in 1810. Court appointed Margaret
Kentlemyres as her guardian in 1810.

KENTLEMYRES, JOHN HENRY, age 15 on March 5, 1810. Court appointed
Margaret Kentlemyres as his guardian in 1810.

KENTLEMYRES, MARGARET, guardian of Nancy Kentlemyres, Harriot
Kentlemyres, John Henry Kentlemyres, and Alexander Kentlemyres
in 1810.

KENTLEMYRES, NANCY, age 13 in 1810. Court appointed Margaret
Kentlemyres as her guardian in 1810.

KERR, EDWARD, master of Negro Magaret in 1810 indenture.

KERR, JAMES, master of Phebe Singleton (daughter of John
Singleton) in 1809 indenture.

KERR, JAMES, master of Thomas Johnson in 1815 indenture.

KERR, ROBERT JR., master of Negro Sam (orphan) in 1820 indenture.

KEYS, JAMES (son of James Keys, Sr.), age 19 on October 9, 1804,
was indentured to John S. Peck & Co. in 1805 to learn to be a
tanner.

KEYS, JAMES SR., father of James Keys in 1805 indenture.

KIDD, JAMES, age 17 on May 8, 1817. Court recognized Penselia
    Kidd as his natural guardian in 1817.
KIDD, PENSELD, master of Negro Benjamin in 1816 indenture.
KIDD, PENSELIA, natural guardian of James Kidd in 1817.
KIMBALL, WILLIAM (orphan), age 16 in May, 1829, was indentured to
    Joseph C. Carver in 1829 to learn to be a blacksmith.
KIMBERLY, MARTHA, age 9 in October, 1808. Court appointed Joshua
    Dulaney as her guardian in 1808.
KIMBERLY, POLLY, age 15 in October, 1807. Court appointed Joshua
    Dulaney as her guardian in 1808.
KIMBLE, GEORGE (son of Stephen Kimble, deceased), age 12 on
    October 8, 1807, was indentured to Samuel Everest in 1808 to
    learn to be a taylor.
KIMBLE, JAMES, age 17 on May 8, 1813. Court appointed Hannah
    Armstrong as his guardian in 1813.
KIMBLE, JOHN, age 15 in February, 1814. Court appointed Hannah
    Armstrong as his guardian in 1813, and he was then indentured
    to John Dunken in 1813 to learn to be a coach maker.
KIMBLE, MERANDA, age 10 in February, 1814. Court appointed Hannah
    Armstrong as her guardian in 1813.
KIMBLE, STEPHEN, age 12 in April, 1813. Court appointed Hannah
    Armstrong as his guardian in 1813, and he was then indentured
    to Bennett Stewart in 1813 to learn to be a tanner and
    currier.
KIMBLE, STEPHEN, deceased father of George Kimble in 1808
    indenture.
KIRK, JAMES, master of Charles F. Bruce in 1809 indenture.
KIRK, WILLIAM, master of Charles Henry in 1815 indenture.
KIRKWOOD, JEBEZ, guardian of James Thompson in 1821.
KIRKWOOD, ROBERT SR., master of Eliza Jane Hughes in 1827
    indenture.
KIRKWOOD, WILLIAM C., master of Edward Cole in 1828 indenture.
KITHCART, WILLIAM, master of Robert Mallock in 1807 indenture.
KITHCART, WILLIAM, master of Parker Ruth in 1808 indenture.
KNIGHT, ANN, mother of Robert Knight in 1815 indenture.
KNIGHT, GEORGE (orphan), age 14 on May 1, 1821, was indentured
    with the consent of "his sister, Sharlota Hamilton, his
    nearest living relative," to Isaac Hoopman in 1821 to learn to
    be a cooper.
KNIGHT, HENRY, age 15 on October 9, 1801, was indentured to Scott
    Hughes in 1802 to learn to be a tanner and currier.
KNIGHT, ROBERT (son of Ann Knight), age 15 in October, 1815, was
    indentured to William Hunter, Jr. in 1815 to learn to be a
    taylor.
LAKE, AMOS, guardian of Jesse Lake (son of Hannah Lake) in 1817.
LAKE, AMOS, master of John Woods in 1821 indenture.
LAKE, HANNAH, mother of Jesse Lake in 1817 guardianship.
LAKE, JESSE (son of Hannah Lake), age 17 in April, 1817. Court
    appointed Amos Lake as his guardian in 1817.
LAMBORN, DANIEL, master of John McCarty (son of James McCarty)
    and David Norris (son of Jesse Norris) in 1820 indentures.
LAMMOTT, BARBARY, guardian of Moses Lammott, Levi Lammott, Joshua
    Lammott, and Katherine Lammott in 1801.
LAMMOTT, JOSHUA, no age given in 1801, chose Barbary Lammott as
    his guardian in 1801.

LAMMOTT, KATHERINE, no age given in 1801, chose Barbary Lammott as her guardian in 1801.

LAMMOTT, LEVI, age 14 in 1801, chose Barbary Lammott as his guardian in 1801.

LAMMOTT, MOSES, age about 16 in 1801, chose Barbary Lammott as his guardian in 1801.

LANE, JOHN, master of Ann Jones (daughter of Frances Jones) in 1803 indenture.

LANE, JOHN, one of the guardians of Mary McKinnon, Michael McKinnon, Thomas McKinnon, and Rachel McKinnon in 1811.

LAWRENCE, JOHN, age 15 on August 12, 1802, was indentured to Aquila McComas in 1802 to learn to be a house carpenter and joiner.

LAWSON, ALEXANDER, age 18 in April, 1808. Court appointed Edward Griffith as his guardian in 1808.

LEACH, JAMES, master of Negro Mariah in 1803 indenture.

LEASTATER, THOMAS (orphan), age 13 on August 30, 1825, was indentured "with the consent of Elijah Waskey and his friends" to Stephen A. Peerce on August 21, 1826, to learn to be a hatter.

LEE (Negro, illegitimate), age 1 month on June 21, 1813, was indentured to William Price in 1813 to learn to be a farmer.

LEE, DAVID, master of Negro Isaac in 1801 indenture.

LEE, HENRY H., age 16 on June 9, 1829. Court appointed Mary Lee as his guardian in 1829.

LEE, JAMES C., age 12 on March 28, 1830. Court appointed Mary Lee as his guardian in 1830.

LEE, LOYD, master of Negro Elizor in 1813 indenture.

LEE, MARSHALL, master of Hugh McGonegall in 1808 indenture.

LEE, MARY, guardian of Henry H. Lee and James C. Lee in 1829.

LEE, RALPH, master of Elias Butler (Negro) in 1821 indenture.

LEE, RALPH, master of Charity Cowan (Negro) in 1806 indenture.

LEE, RALPH S., master of Elias Butler (Negro) in 1820 indenture.

LEE, RALPH S., master of Joel Benson in 1824 indenture.

LEE, RALPH SACKETT, master of Abraham Hilton (Negro) in 1804 indenture.

LEE, RALPH SACKETT, master of William Cole (orphan) in 1816 indenture.

LEE, WILLIAM D., guardian of Elizabeth P. Bryarly and Wakeman Bryarly (children of Dr. Wakeman Bryarly) in 1821.

LENNEN, ANN, guardian of Frances Helen Lennen in 1807.

LENNEN, FRANCES HELEN, age 4 months on September 18, 1807. Court appointed Ann Lennen as her guardian in 1807.

LESTER, WILLIAM, guardian of Martha Browning in 1803.

LEVIN [LEWIN?], JOHN, master of Eli Rhodes (son of Hannah Rhodes) in 1801 indenture.

LEWIS (Negro son of Negro Sarah), no age given in 1817, was indentured with the consent of his mother to Cunningham Whiteford in 1817 to learn to be a farmer.

LEWIS (Negro), age 12 on September 1, 1805, was indentured with the consent of his mother (not named) to James Taylor in 1806 to learn to be a bay craft sailor.

LEWIS, ELI, age 16 on January 12, 1804, was indentured to Joshua Husbands in 1804 to learn to be a tanner and currier.

LILLEY, HENRY, guardian of Thomas Lilley in 1812.

LILLEY, THOMAS, age 6 on October 3, 1811. Court appointed Henry
Liley as his guardian in 1812.

LINDA (Negro), mother of Negro Watkins in 1801 indenture.

LINDAY (Negro), age about 60 in 1823, valued at $30, and formerly
owned by William Calwell, deceased, in October, 1823.

LINDEY (Negro), age 12 on August 1, 1809, was indentured to
Francis Mechen in 1809 to learn to do housework.

LINOM [LYNUM], ANN, mother of Susanna Lynum [Linom] in 1802
indenture.

LINOM [LYNUM], SUSANNA (daughter of Ann Linom or Lynum), age 16
on October 25, 1808, was indentured to William Quarll in 1802
to learn to do housework.

LOGUE, JAMES, master of John Thomas (Colored) in 1828 indenture.

LONDON (Negro), age 12 on December 1, 1825, was indentured with
the consent of his mother (not named) to Samuel Worthington in
1826 to learn to be a farmer.

LONEY, ALSE, wife of Amos Loney, deceased, and mother of Thomas
Loney and Mary Ann Loney in 1811 indentures.

LONEY, AMOS, husband of Alse Loney and deceased father of Thomas
Loney and Mary Ann Loney in 1811 indentures.

LONEY, MARY ANN (daughter of Amos Loney, deceased), age 12 on
August 6, 1811, "abandoned by her mother, Alse Loney," was
indentured to Joseph Wiggins in 1811 to learn to do housework.

LONEY, MARY, by her will, freed Negro Ephraim on April 1, 1826.

LONEY, THOMAS (son of Amos Loney, deceased), age 16 on January
13, 1811, "abandoned by his mother, Alse Loney," was
indentured to Joseph Wiggins in 1811 to learn to be a cabinet
maker.

LONG, ABRAHAM (son of John Long), age 17 on March 1, 1808, was
indentured with the consent of his father to John Davis in
1808 to learn to be a boot and shoemaker.

LONG, AQUILA, age 17 on November 6, 1806, was indentured to
Aquila McComas (son of James McComas) in 1807.

LONG, JOHN, father of Abraham Long in 1808 indenture.

LOUIS, HENRY (freeborn Negro of Mary Donaldson), born July 8,
1812, was indentured to James C. Doddrell on August 15, 1827,
to learn to be a farmer.

LOW, ALICE ANN, natural guardian of John Clark Low, Jeremiah Low,
Kesiah Low, and Hannah Low in 1817.

LOW, HANNAH, age 1 on July 26, 1816. Court recognized Alice Ann
Low as her natural guardian in 1817.

LOW, JEREMIAH, age 5 in April, 1816. Court recognized Alice Ann
Low as his natural guardian in 1817.

LOW, JOHN CLARK, age 7 on March 17, 1816. Court recognized Alice
Ann Low as his natural guardian in 1817.

LOW, KESIAH, age 3 on June 4, 1816. Court recognized Alice Ann
Low as her natural guardian in 1817.

LUCANS, ELY, master of Frederic Levi Foster (son of John Foster)
in 1806.

LUCKIE, JOHN, master of Joseph Townsley in 1802 indenture.

LUKENS, BENJAMIN (son of Jacob Lukens), no age given in 1804, was
indentured to Benjamin Brindley in 1804 to learn to be a wagon
maker.

LUKENS, BENJAMIN, master of John Maddin in 1818 indenture.

LUKENS, BENJAMIN, master of William Carr in 1821 indenture.

LUKENS, CHARLES (son of Jacob Lukens), no age given in 1807, was
indentured to David Maulsby (son of John Maulsby) to learn to
be a blacksmith.

LUKENS, JACOB, father of Benjamin Lukens in 1804 indenture.

LUKENS, JACOB, father of Charles Lukens in 1807 indenture.

LYNUM, SUSANNA, see "Susanna Linom [Lynum]," q.v., in 1802.

LYTLE, AMBROSE (orphan), age 14 on June 8, 1828, was indentured
to John Rouse in 1828 to learn to be a farmer.

LYTLE, BENJAMIN (son of George Lytle, Jr.), age 10 in August,
1821. Court appointed Cornelius Cole as his guardian in 1821.

LYTLE, GEORGE JR., father of Susan Lytle, Benjamin Lytle, and
Joseph Lytle in 1821 guardianships.

LYTLE, JAMES, master of Morris Ingram Burk (son of James Burk) in
1803 indenture.

LYTLE, JANE, age 10 in April, 1815. Court appointed Clark Hollis
as her guardian in 1815.

LYTLE, JOSEPH (son of George Lytle, Jr.), age 7 in August, 1821.
Court appointed Cornelius Cole as his guardian in 1821.

LYTLE, LOISA [sic], "illegitimate female," age 7 on November 27,
1827, was indentured to Samuel Ecoff in 1828 to learn to do
housework.

LYTLE, SUSAN (daughter of George Lytle, Jr.), age 13 in August,
1821. Court appointed Cornelius Cole as her guardian in 1821.

MACATEE, CLEMENT, deceased husband of Rebecka Macatee, father of
Mary Ann Macatee and George Macatee, and brother of Capt.
Henry Macatee, in 1824 indenture.

MACATEE, GEORGE, son of Clement (deceased) and Rebecka Macatee,
age 12 on March 17, 1824. (When Rebecka Macatee refused to
accept his guardianship it was assigned to Capt. Henry
Macatee, an uncle of George Macatee, on November 30, 1824).

MACATEE, HENRY (Captain), brother of Clement Macatee (deceased by
1824) and guardian of Mary Ann Macatee and George Macatee
(children of Clement and Rebecka Macatee) in 1824.

MACATEE, MARY ANN, daughter of Clement (deceased) and Rebecka
Macatee, age 14 on January 10, 1824. (When Rebecka Macatee
refused to accept her guardianship it was assigned to Capt.
Henry Macatee, an uncle of Mary Ann Macatee, on November 30,
1824).

MACATEE, REBECKA, widow of Clement Macatee and mother of Mary Ann
Macatee and George Macatee in 1824 guardianship (which was
assigned to Capt. Henry Macatee, her brother-in-law, in 1824).

MACATEE, SAMUEL, guardian of Rachel Ann Quinlan, Philip Thomas
Quinlan, Charity Quinlan, and Charles Quinlan in 1823.

MACKENTIRE, REBECCA, "age about 12" in 1802, was indentured to
William Wilson (silversmith) in 1802 to learn to do housework.

MACKIE, BENJAMIN (orphan), age 16 on January 3, 1805, was
indentured to George W. Bradford in 1805 to learn to be a
hatter.

MADDEN, COMFORT, wife of James Madden in 1802 indenture.

MADDEN, JAMES AND COMFORT (his wife), masters of Jenny Bradford
(Negro) and James Bradford (Negro) in 1802 indentures.

MADDEN, JAMES, master of Thomas Burrass in 1823 indenture.

MADDEN, JAMES, master of John Madden in 1820 indenture.

MADDEN, JOHN (orphan), age 18 in January, 1820, was indentured to
James Madden in 1820 to learn to be a plasterer.

MADDEN, JOSEPH, age 18 on December 1, 1824, was indentured with
the consent of his mother (not named) to Harmon Thomas in 1824
to learn to be a boot and shoemaker.

MADDIN, JOHN (orphan), age 15 on January 1, 1818, was indentured
to Benjamin Lukens in 1818 to learn to be a wheelwright.

MADDON, HENRY (orphan), age 15 on November 15, 1825, was
indentured "with the consent of his friends" to William
Bradford in 1826 to learn to be a hatter.

MAGNESS, JOHN, age 15 on September 1, 1823, was indentured with
the consent of his father (not named) to John McClure in 1823
to learn to be a boot and shoemaker.

MAGNESS, JOHN, guardian of John Morris and Loyd Morris in 1802.

MAGNESS, JOHN, master of Negro Tower in 1822 indenture.

MAHAN, BENJAMIN, master of James Townsley (orphan) in 1808
indenture.

MAHAN, GEORGE (son of Sarah Mahan, of Cecil County, Maryland), no
age given in 1803, was indentured to John Donn, of Havre de
Grace, Maryland, in 1803 to learn to be a coach maker.

MAHAN, SARAH (of Cecil County), mother of George Mahan in 1803
indenture.

MAHON, JOHN SR., guardian of John Townsley, Joseph Townsley,
James Townsley, and William Townsley in 1802.

MAHON, LAZARUS, master of Hugh Gunnion (son of Hugh Gunnion) in
1803 indenture.

MALLOCK, ROBERT (son of Susannah Mallock), age 4 on March 10,
1806, was indentured to William Kithcart in 1806 to learn to
be a farmer.

MALLOCK, SUSANNAH, mother of Robert Mallock in 1806 indenture.

MALSBY, DAVID, guardian of the children of the late James Johnson
(Milton Johnson, John Johnson, Thomas Johnson, Robert Johnson,
Hannah Johnson, Chany [Chancy?] Johnson, Joseph Johnson, Sarah
Johnson, Ely Johnson, Mary Ann Johnson, and Pheba Johnson) in
1821.

MALSBY, DAVID, master of Henry Dorsey (son of Mathew Dorsey) in
1809 indenture.

MALSBY, MORRIS, master of Stephen Aselin (orphan) in 1809
indenture.

MALSBY, MORRIS, master of Harriet Brazier in 1813 indenture.

MANAHAN, ELIZABETH, see "Elizabeth Monahan," q.v., in 1810.

MANSFIELD, RICHARD AND ANN, masters of Margaret Walker in 1812
indenture.

MARAN, WILLIAM (destitute orphan), age 16 on December 1, 1822,
was indentured to John Sterett in 1823 to learn to be a shoe
and boot maker.

MARGARET (Negro, illegitimate), age 12 in August, 1809, was
indentured with the consent of her mother (not named) to
Edward Kerr in 1810 to learn to do housework.

MARGARET (Negro), mother of Negro Richard in 1803 indenture.

MARIAH (Negro), age 5 in 1803, was indentured with the consent of
her mother (not named) to James Leach in 1803 to learn to do
housework.

MARSH, THOMAS, age 15 on December 15, 1814, was indentured with
the consent of his mother (not named) to William Careins in
1814 to learn to be a spinning wheelwright.

MARSHALL, SAMUEL, master of Elijah Tayson (orphan) in 1808

indenture.

MARTIN, ANDREW, master of Negro Tower in 1809 indenture.

MARTIN, HENRY (Negro orphan), age 5 on May 23, 1827, was indentured to John H. Eaton in 1827 to learn to be a rough carpenter.

MARTIN, MOSES (Colored), "now age 21 and bound to William Richardson, is now free, December 28, 1824."

MARTIN, MOSES (Negro), age 12 on May 10, 1813, was indentured to William Richardson in 1813 to learn to be a farmer.

MARTIN, ROBERT, master of Negro Fanny in 1821 indenture.

MARY (Negro), mother of Negro Jack in 1805 indenture.

MARY (Negro), now age 35 in 1829, was to be freed by the will of Thomas Bond in 1800 when she became 25 (recorded June 2, 1829).

MARY ANN (Negro, illegitimate), age 4 on September 1, 1827, was indentured with the consent of her mother (not named) to Richard Cole in 1828 to learn to do housewifery.

MARY ANN (Negro), "a bright Mulatto and illegitimate child," age 2 on December 4, 1808, was indentured to John Cunningham in 1809 to learn to do housework.

MARY ANN (Negro), age 9 on July 15, 1815, was indentured with the consent of her mother (not named) to Elizabeth Diver in 1816 to learn to do housework.

MASON, HOWARD, master of Jonathan Howard (orphan) in 1824 indenture.

MASSEY, AQUILA B., master of Negro Hannah and Negro Hampton in 1825 indenture.

MASSEY, AQUILA, guardian of William Barnes in 1806 "in room of Samuel Rea who has left this state."

MASSEY, AQUILA, master of Negro John (orphan) in 1820 indenture.

MATHER, THOMAS, master of Caiphus Bond (Negro) in 1822 indenture.

MATHEWS, JOHN C., age 12 on April 15, 1810. Court appointed Benedict Hanson as his guardian in 1810.

MATHEWS, MARY ELIZABETH, age 8 on April 19, 1810. Court appointed Benedict Hanson as her guardian in 1810.

MATHEWS, MARY FRANCES, age 4 on June 19, 1810. Court appointed Benedict Hanson as her guardian in 1810.

MATHEWS, MILKEY L., age 10 on February 28, 1810. Court appointed Benedict Hanson as her guardian in 1810.

MATHEWS, WILLIAM L., age 6 on April 29, 1810. Court appointed Benedict Hanson as his guardian in 1810.

MATILDA (Negro), age 2 on May 15, 1818, was indentured to William Taylor in 1818 to learn to do housework.

MAULSBY, DAVID (son of John Maulsby), master of Charles Lukens in 1807 indenture.

MAULSBY, DAVID, age 17 on May 10, 1801, was indentured to Maurice Maulsby in 1801 to learn to be a blacksmith.

MAULSBY, DAVID, master of Negro Abraham in 1806 indenture.

MAULSBY, DAVID, master of Solomon Foard (orphan) in 1811 indenture.

MAULSBY, ELEANOR, guardian of Elizabeth Maulsby in 1802.

MAULSBY, ELIZABETH, age 10 in 1802. Court appointed Eleanor Maulsby as her guardian in 1802.

MAULSBY, FRANCES, master of Negro Patty in 1818 indenture.

MAULSBY, ISRAEL D., guardian of Ameline Hitchcock, Jason

Hitchcock, Elizabeth Hitchcock, Luther Hitchcock, Jarrett Hitchcock, and Dennis Hitchcock in 1809.

MAULSBY, ISRAEL D., master of Negro George in 1809 indenture.

MAULSBY, JOHN, father of David Maulsby in 1807 record.

MAULSBY, MAURICE, master of David Maulsby, and Negro Watkins (son of Negro Linda) in 1801 indenture.

MAULSBY, MORRIS, master of Ezekiel Jones (orphan) in 1804 indenture.

MAULSBY, MORRIS, master of Abraham Parsons in 1816 indenture.

MAULSBY, MORRIS, master of James Norris (son of James Norris) in 1815 indenture.

MAXWELL, ANN ELIZABETH, age 8 on May 12, 1806. Court appointed Ann Maxwell as her guardian in 1807.

MAXWELL, ANN, guardian of Ann Elizabeth Maxwell and James Lambert Maxwell in 1807.

MAXWELL, JAMES LAMBERT, age 6 on September 15, 1806. Court appointed Ann Maxwell as his guardian in 1807.

MAYS, GEORGE (Colored), born November 17, 1810, was indentured with the consent of his father (not named) to Skipwith H. Coale on August 4, 1826, to learn to be a farmer.

McADOW, ANDREW, guardian of William Edges in 1804.

McCARTY, DANIEL (orphan), age 13 on June 3, 1823, was indentured with the consent of his mother, Mary McCarty, to Francis Johns of Abingdon, Maryland, in 1823, to learn to be a boot and shoemaker.

McCARTY, JAMES (of Chester County, Pennsylvania), father of John McCarty in 1820 indenture in Harford County, Maryland.

McCARTY, JOHN (son of James McCarty, of Chester County, Pennsylvania), age 17 on October 7, 1819, was indentured to Daniel Lamborn in 1820 to learn to be a paper maker.

McCARTY, MARY, mother of Daniel McCarty in 1823 indenture.

McCLANNON, ELEANOR (orphan), age 10 on November 3, 1803, was indentured to Joseph Jay in 1804 to learn to do housework.

McCLUNG, ROBERT, master of Belinda Hitchcock in 1827 indenture.

McCLUNG, ROBERT, master of Billender Hitchcock in 1828 indenture.

McCLURE, JOHN, master of John Magness in 1823 indenture.

McCOMAS, ALEXANDER, master of Samuel Adams (Negro) in 1814 indenture.

McCOMAS, ALEXANDER, master of James Henry (Negro) in 1816 indenture.

McCOMAS, AMOS, master of Davis Carman (son of Andrew Carman) in 1806.

McCOMAS, ANN B., age 12 in August, 1825. Court appointed Elizabeth McComas as her guardian in 1826.

McCOMAS, AQUILA (son of James McComas), master of Aquila Long in 1807 indenture.

McCOMAS, AQUILA, master of Lee Wilson in 1802 indenture.

McCOMAS, AQUILA, master of William Norris in 1809 indenture.

McCOMAS, AQUILA, master of James Chocke in 1811 indenture.

McCOMAS, AQUILA, master of Aquila Hitchcock (son of Charity Hitchcock) until October 16, 1805.

McCOMAS, AQUILA SCOTT (orphan), age 15 on June 19, 1816, was indentured to Daniel Cunningham in 1817 to learn to be a house carpenter.

McCOMAS, BARNET, master of Negro Freeborn in 1803 indenture.

McCOMAS, DANIEL, father of John McComas in 1806 indenture.
McCOMAS, ELIZABETH, guardian of Thomas B. McComas, Mary Maria
   McComas, and Ann B. McComas in 1826.
McCOMAS, JAMES, father of Aquila McComas in 1807 indenture.
McCOMAS, JAMES S., master of Negro Josias in 1819 indenture.
McCOMAS, JAMES S., master of Milton Johnson and John Johnson in
   1820 indentures.
McCOMAS, JAMES S., master of Aquila Duley in 1812 indenture.
McCOMAS, JAMES S., master of Francis Standish Everist in 1811
   indenture.
McCOMAS, JAMES S., master of Thomas Johnson in 1823.
McCOMAS, JOHN (son of Daniel McComas), age 19 in June, 1805.
   Court appointed Josias Scott McComas as his guardian in 1806.
McCOMAS, JOHN, master of Negro Abraham in 1819 indenture.
McCOMAS, JOHN W., master of Robert Whiteford (orphan) in 1809
   indenture.
McCOMAS, JOSIAS S., guardian of Charity Gough in 1811.
McCOMAS, JOSIAS SCOTT, master of William Carter in 1806
   indenture.
McCOMAS, JOSIAS SCOTT, guardian of John McComas (son of Daniel
   McComas) in 1806.
McCOMAS, MARY MARIA, age 17 on February 5, 1826. Court appointed
   Elizabeth McComas as her guardian in 1826.
McCOMAS, MOSES S. (orphan), age 16 on December 5, 1814, was
   indentured to Howell Mitchell in 1815 to learn to be a
   blacksmith.
McCOMAS, ROBERT, master of Richard Garrett in 1814 indenture.
McCOMAS, THOMAS B., age 15 on May 17, 1826. Court appointed
   Elizabeth McComas as his guardian in 1826.
McCOMAS, WILLIAM, master of William Paca and Lloyd Riley in 1828
   indentures.
McCONNELL, SAMUEL, master of George Washington (Negro) and Mary
   Jane Wilmer (Negro) in 1820 indentures.
McCOWAN, MICHAEL, master of Jerrard Moore in 1809 indenture.
McCOWEN, CHARLOTTE, mother of Edward McCowen in 1823 indenture.
McCOWEN, EDWARD (orphan son of Charlotte McCowen), age 9 on
   December 1, 1822, was indentured to Alexander Boid in 1823 to
   learn to be a farmer and weaver.
McCRACKEN, JOHN, master of John Pennix in 1801 indenture.
McCULLOUGH, BENJAMIN (son of Robert McCullough), age 15 on June
   15, 1806, was indentured to Thomas Proctor in 1806 to learn to
   be a slater.
McCULLOUGH, ROBERT, father of Benjamin McCullough in 1806
   indenture.
McFADDIN, JOHN, master of Robert Crissee in 1827 indenture.
McGAW, JAMES, master of Negro Thomas in 1803 indenture.
McGONEGAL, DANIEL, father of Hugh McGonegal in 1811 indenture.
McGONEGAL, HUGH, "age 10 or 11" in August, 1811, "abandoned by
   his father, Daniel McGonegal," was indentured to John Jordon
   in 1811 to learn to be a weaver.
McGONEGALL, DANIEL, age 6 on August 16, 1808, was indentured with
   the consent of his father (not named) to William Cronin in
   1808 to learn to be a cooper.
McGONEGALL, HUGH, age 8 on September 22, 1808, was indentured
   with the consent of his father (not named) to Marshall Lee in

1808 to learn to be a cordwainer.

McJILTON, WILLIAM, master of Hugh Gladden in 1808 indenture.

McJILTON, WILLIAM, master of William Barnes (orphan) in 1805 indenture.

McKAN [McKAM?], DANIEL, son of Kitty McKan (McKam?), age 13 years, 11 months and 12 days on November 30, 1810, was indentured to Isaac Smith in 1810 to learn to be a miller.

McKAN [McKAM?], KITTY, mother of Daniel McKan (McKam?) in 1810 indenture.

McKENNEY, JOHN, master of Samuel Stallion in 1803 indenture.

McKINNON, MARY, age 12 on August 11, 1811. Court appointed William Whiteford and John Lane as her guardians in 1811.

McKINNON, MICHAEL, age 7 on January 6, 1811. Court appointed William Whiteford and John Lane as his guardians in 1811.

McKINNON, RACHEL, age 3 on March 22, 1811. Court appointed William Whiteford and John Lane as her guardians in 1811.

McKINNON, THOMAS, age 6 on September 1, 1811. Court appointed William Whiteford and John Lane as his guardians in 1811.

McLAUGHLIN, DANIEL, father of John McLaughlin in 1808 indenture.

McLAUGHLIN, JOHN (son of Daniel McLaughlin), no age given in 1808, was indentured to George Bartol in 1808 to learn to be a baker and grocer.

McLAUGHLIN, PATRICK, master of Leveridge Way in 1805 indenture.

McMATH, WILLIAM, master of Negro Henary in 1812 indenture.

McMURRAY, MARGARET, mother of Richard McMurray in 1802 indenture.

McMURRAY, RICHARD, age 16 on July 20, 1801, was indentured with the consent of his mother, Margaret McMurray, to Benjamin Duberry in May, 1801, to learn to be a wagon maker or wheelwright (Indenture was recorded in 1802).

McNULTY, JANE, age 7 in March, 1829, was indentured with the consent of her mother (not named) to Henry Whitamore in 1829 to learn to be a housekeeper.

MECHEM, FRANCIS, master of Negro Lindey in 1809 indenture.

MEEKS, ALCE [sic], age 13 on May 1, 1810. Court appointed Isaiah Taylor as her guardian in 1810.

MEEKS, CHARLOTTE, age 11 on December 25, 1809. Court appointed Isaiah Taylor as her guardian in 1810.

MEEKS, WILLIAM, age 17 on March 3, 1820, was indentured with the consent of his guardian, William Trager, to George Crevensten in 1820 to learn to be a blacksmith.

MEEKS, WILLIAM, age 8 on March 3, 1810. Court appointed Isaiah Taylor as his guardian in 1810.

MELVINA (Negro), age 5 on June 5, 1822, was indentured with the consent of her mother (not named) to Samuel and Elizabeth Cox in 1822 to learn to be a servant.

MICHAEL (Negro boy), no age given in May, 1822, was indentured with the consent of his mother (not named) to Jason Moore to learn to be a farmer ("formerly bound to Thomas Shay on December 12, 1814, but he lately died, leaving no widow").

MICHAEL, JACOB, guardian of Mary Greenfield, Joseph Greenfield, Martha Greenfield, Henry Austin Greenfield, Jacob Greenfield, and Elizabeth Greenfield in 1805. [Note: Record first states guardian is Jacob Michael and then it states guardian is Jacob Greenfield].

MICHAEL, JACOB, master of Thomas Grant in 1803 indenture.

MICHAEL, JAMES AND NEOMAH, masters of Negro Juda in 1801
indenture.
MICHAEL, MATILDA, age 6 on November 15, 1816. Court recognized
Neomi Michael as her natural guardian in 1817.
MICHAEL, NEOMI, natural guardian of William Michael, Susan
Michael, and Matilda Michael in 1817.
MICHAEL, SUSAN, age 8 on September 16, 1817. Court recognized
Neomi Michael as her natural guardian in 1817.
MICHAEL, WILLIAM, age 13 in August, 1817. Court recognized Neoni
Michael as his natural guardian in 1817.
MICHAEL, WILLIAM, master of John Washington Peters in 1828
indenture.
MIDDLEDITCH, MARY ANN, aged 11 months and 17 days in March [?],
1814, was indentured with the consent of her mother (not
named) to Martha Harrid [sic] in 1813 to learn to do
housework.
MIDDLETON, MAULDEN G., guardian of Ann R. Spencer and Emarlia
[Emaulis?] Spencer in 1816.
MIDDLETON, SARAH ELIZABETH, age 13 on December 20, 1828. Court
appointed William Murphy as her guardian on December 30, 1828.
MIDDLETON, WILLIAM HENRY, age 14 on August 20, 1828. Court
appointed William Murphy as his guardian on December 30, 1828.
MIDHALF, ABRAHAM, master of Stephen Cohee in 1815 indenture.
MIKE (Negro), age 12 in December, 1814, was indentured to Thomas
Shay in 1813 to learn to be a farmer.
MILES, AQUILA, master of Negro Ruth in 1815 indenture.
MILLER, ADELINE, age 14 on January 11, 1816. Court appointed
William F. Miller as her guardian in 1816.
MILLER, ADELINE, age 13 on January 6, 1815. Court appointed
Edward Miller as her guardian in 1815.
MILLER, ANN, age 8 in May, 1801. Court appointed Margaret Miller
as her guardian in 1801.
MILLER, EDWARD, age 2 on December 23, 1814. Court appointed
Edward Miller as his guardian in 1814.
MILLER, EDWARD, age 3 on December 2, 1815. Court appointed
William F. Miller as his guardian in 1816.
MILLER, EDWARD, guardian of Adeline Miller, Horatio Miller,
Joseph Miller, Thomas Miller, and Edward Miller in 1815.
MILLER, EDWARD, guardian of William Franklin Miller in 1805.
MILLER, EDWARD, guardian of John Miller (son of Joseph Miller) in
1801.
MILLER, EDWARD, master of Negro Sarah in 1806 indenture.
MILLER, HENRY, age 2 in Januaey, 1801. Court appointed Joshua
Husbands as his guardian in 1801.
MILLER, HORATIO, age 10 on February 22, 1815. Court appointed
Edward Miller as his guardian in 1815.
MILLER, HORATIO, age 11 on April 8, 1816. Court appointed William
F. Miller as his guardian in 1816.
MILLER, JOHN (son of Joseph Miller), age 12 in January, 1801.
Court appointed Edward Miller as his guardian in 1801.
MILLER, JOHN (son of Richard Miller), age 11 on May 6, 1827, was
indentured to Samuel C. Stump in 1827 to learn to be a farmer.
MILLER, JOSEPH, age 9 on February 23, 1816. Court appointed
William F. Miller as his guardian in 1816.
MILLER, JOSEPH, age 6 on March 6, 1815. Court appointed Edward

Miller as his guardian in 1815.

MILLER, JOSEPH, deceased, manumitted Negro Jane prior to 1806.

MILLER, JOSEPH, father of John Miller in 1801 guardianship.

MILLER, MARGARET, guardian of Ann Miller in 1801.

MILLER, RICHARD (son of Richard Miller), age 10 on May 19, 1827, was indentured to Thomas C. Stump in 1827 to learn to be a farmer.

MILLER, RICHARD, father of John Miller and Richard Miller in 1827 indentures.

MILLER, THOMAS, age 5 on April 23, 1815. Court appointed Edward Miller as his guardian in 1815.

MILLER, THOMAS C., age 5 on March 6, 1816. Court appointed William F. Miller as his guardian in 1816.

MILLER, THOMAS CHEW, age 17 on December 13, 1800. Court appointed Thomas Chew as his guardian in 1801.

MILLER, WILLIAM, age 10 in March, 1801. Court appointed Thomas Jay as his guardian in 1801.

MILLER, WILLIAM F., guardian of Adeline Miller, Horatio Miller, Joseph Miller, Thomas C. Miller, and Edward Miller in 1816.

MILLER, WILLIAM FRANKLIN, age 14 in March, 1805. Court appointed Edward Miller as his guardian in 1805.

MILLER, WILLIAM, master of Elisha Wood in 1815 indenture.

MILLHOOF, JOHN, master of John Dennison (son of William Dennison) in 1818 indenture.

MILLS, THOMAS, master of Margaret Gorden in 1817 indenture.

MILLS, WILLIAM, master of Luther Hitchcock (son of Esther Hitchcock) in 1815 indenture.

MITCHELL, BENEDICT EDWARD, age 8 on July 4, 1807. Court appointed Susanna Mitchell as his guardian in 1807.

MITCHELL, BENEDICT EDWARD (orphan), age 18 on July 4, 1817, was indentured with the consent of his mother (not named) to Edward Mitchell in 1817 to learn to be a wagon maker.

MITCHELL, CLEMENCY, age 12 on April 3, 1813. Court appointed Sarah Mitchell as her guardian in 1813.

MITCHELL, DANIEL, age 5 on May 4, 1807. Court appointed Susanna Mitchell as his guardian in 1807.

MITCHELL, EDWARD, master of Benedict Edward Mitchell in 1817 indenture.

MITCHELL, EVAN, age 5 on November 9, 1812. Court appointed Sarah Mitchell as his guardian in 1813.

MITCHELL, HARRIOT, age 11 in December, 1806. Court appointed Susanna Mitchell as her guardian in 1807.

MITCHELL, HIXON, age 10 on February 21, 1813. Court appointed Sarah Mitchell as his guardian in 1813.

MITCHELL, HOWELL, master of Moses S. McComas (orphan) in 1815 indenture.

MITCHELL, HOWELL, master of John Stratten in 1818 indenture.

MITCHELL, JAMES, age 15 on November 18, 1808, was indentured to George England in 1809 to learn to be a farmer.

MITCHELL, JOHN, age 14 on May 7, 1813. Court appointed Sarah Mitchell as his guardian in 1813.

MITCHELL, MAHALAH, age 3 on April 20, 1807. Court appointed Susanna Mitchell as her guardian in 1807.

MITCHELL, NANCY, age 2 on December 10, 1812. Court appointed Sarah Mitchell as her guardian in 1813.

MITCHELL, NANCY, age 13 in December, 1806. Court appointed
   Susanna Mitchell as her guardian in 1807.
MITCHELL, PARKER, age 8 on May 13, 1813. Court appointed Sarah
   Mitchell as his guardian in 1813.
MITCHELL, RICHARD, age 17 on October 18, 1821, was indentured
   with the consent of his mother (not named) to James Chesney in
   1821 to learn to be a wheelwright.
MITCHELL, RICHARD, guardian of Ann Martha Mitchell in 1809.
MITCHELL, SARAH, guardian of John Mitchell, Clemency Mitchell,
   Hixon Mitchell, Parker Mitchell, Evan Mitchell, and Nancy
   Mitchell in 1813.
MITCHELL, SUSANNA, guardian of Nancy Mitchell, Harriot Mitchell,
   Benedict Edward Mitchell, Daniel Mitchell, and Mahalah
   Mitchell in 1807.
MONAHAN, ELIZABETH (daughter of Susannah Monahan), age 5 years,
   11 months, and 18 days on May 22, 1810, was indentured to
   George G. Presbury in 1810 to learn to do housework.
MONAHAN, SUSANNAH, mother of Elizabeth Monahan in 1810 indenture.
MONKS, FRANCES E., master of Bennett Oliver in 1815 indenture.
MONKS, FRANCES E., master of Bennett Oliver in 1815 indenture.
MONKS, JOHN, guardian of Martha Browning in 1807.
MONKS, JOHN, master of Negro Gabriel in 1811 indenture.
MONTGOMERY, JOHN (Esquire), master of Negro Samuel in 1802
   indenture.
MONTGOMERY, MARY, master of Cassandra Webster (Negro) in 1809
   indenture.
MONTGOMERY, ROBERT (orphan), age 9 on June 1, 1825, was
   indentured to James Wilson in 1825 to learn to be a cooper.
MONTGOMERY, THOMAS (son of Thomas Montgomery), age 17 on February
   7, 1816, was indentured to William Nevill in 1816 to learn to
   be a blacksmith.
MONTGOMERY, THOMAS, father of Thomas Montgomery in 1816
   indenture.
MONTGOMERY, WILLIAM B., master of Richard Bradford (Mulatto) in
   1821 indenture.
MOOBERRY, WILLIAM (orphan), age 16 years and 6 months on November
   13, 1815, was indentured to John Steel in 1816 to learn to be
   a blacksmith.
MOORE, BARNEY (orphan), age 13 on August 7, 1819, was indentured
   to Isaac Stansbury in 1819 to learn to be a miller.
MOORE, CARVIL, age 9 on March 29, 1819, was indentured to
   Benjamin Gibson in 1820 to learn to be a cooper.
MOORE, JASON, guardian of Sophia Bond Moore, Nancy Bond Moore,
   and Pemelia Bond Moore in 1803.
MOORE, JASON, master of Negro Michael in 1822 indenture.
MOORE, JASON, master of Negro Jane in 1819 indenture.
MOORE, JERRARD, age 10 on March 27, 1809, was indentured with the
   consent of his mother (not named) to Michael McCowan in 1809
   to learn to be a weaver.
MOORE, NANCY BOND, age 8 on July 29, 1803. Court appointed Jason
   Moore as her guardian in 1803.
MOORE, PEMELIA BOND, age 4 on October 30, 1802. Court appointed
   Jason Moore as her guardian in 1803.
MOORE, SOPHIA BOND, age 9 on March 6, 1803. Court appointed Jason
   Moore as her guardian in 1803.

MOORES, AQUILA PACA, one of the masters of Walter Cunningham in 1821 indenture.

MOORES, JOHN, master of John Francis Augustus Holland in 1814 indenture.

MOORES, JOHN, master of Walter Cunningham in 1821 indenture.

MORFORD, JAMES, age 15 in October, 1812, was indentured with the consent of his father (not named) to Upton Reed and Rees Davis, cutlers, in 1812 to learn to be a spade and shovel maker.

MORFORD, JOHN, no age given in 1807, was indentured with the consent of his parents (not named) to John Rouse to learn to be a spinning wheelwright.

MORGAN, EDWARD (Colored), age 7 on March 8, 1824, was indentured with the consent of his mother (not named) to James Deaver in 1824 to learn to be a farmer.

MORGAN, MARGARET, age 15 in 1804. Court appointed Ephraim Hopkins as her guardian in 1804.

MORGAN, PHEBA, master of Negro Benjamin in 1829 indenture.

MORGAN, WILLIAM, by his will, freed Robert Johnson (Negro) in 1826.

MORINGS, AARON (Negro son of Moses Morings), age 10 on February 10, 1805, was indentured to Skipworth Coale and Richard H. Jones in 1805 to learn to be a tanner.

MORINGS, MOSES (Negro), father of Aaron Morings in 1805 indenture.

MORRIS, JOHN, age 14 on January 14, 1802. Court appointed John Magness as his guardian with the consent of his mother (not named) in 1802 [Note: John Morris was a brother of Loyd Morris, age 7].

MORRIS, LLOYD, no age given in 1803, was indentured with the consent of his mother (not named) to William Divers in 1803 to learn to be a cooper.

MORRIS, LOYD, age 7 on November 14, 1801. Court appointed John Magness as his guardian with the consent of his mother (not named) in 1802 [Note: Loyd Morris was a brother of John Morris, age 14].

MORRIS, WILLIAM (Negro, illegitimate), age 3 on September 15, 1818, was indentured with the consent of his mother (not named) to William Amoss (son of Thomas Amoss) in 1818 to learn to be a farmer.

MORRISON, JOHN, master of John Dickson (son of Rachel Dickson) in 1811 indenture.

MORRISON, JOHN, master of John Barclay in 1828 indenture.

MORRISON, MARY (orphan), age 9 on December 13, 1825, was indentured to Phillip Amos in 1826 to learn to do housework.

MOSES (Negro orphan), age 5 in September, 1811, was indentured to Alesanna Kell in 1811 to learn to do housework [as a servant].

MOSES (Negro), age 4 on January 4, 1808, was indentured with the consent of his mother (not named) to Martin T. Gilbert in 1808 to learn to be a farmer.

MOUGHHAN, JOHN, master of Bob Talbott (Negro) in 1805 indenture.

MURPHY, WILLIAM, guardian of William Henry Middleton and Sarah Elizabeth Middleton in 1828.

MURRAY, GEORGE (Negro orphan), age 12 in 1829, was indentured to John Johnson on June 23, 1829, to learn to be a farmer.

MURRY, MICHAEL, age about 15 in February, 1824, was indentured with the consent of his mother (not named) to Joseph Bosley in 1823 to learn a trade [not specified in record].

NABB, CATHERINE S. (orphan of William Nabb), age 3 on December 20, 1814. Court appointed Thomas W. Bond as her guardian in 1815.

NABB, ELISHA, age 18 on March 4, 1811. Court appointed Thomas Spencer as his guardian in 1811.

NABB, JOHN, age 20 on April 15, 1811. Court appointed Thomas Spencer as his guardian in 1811.

NANCY (Negro), age 7 on May 1, 1816, was indentured with the consent of her mother (not named) to Samuel Hopkins in 1816.

NEALL, HENRY C., master of Hannah Johnes (Negro) in 1825 indenture.

NED (Negro), age about 12 in 1823, valued at $175, and formerly owned by William Calwell, deceased, in October, 1823.

NED (Negro), age 5 on April 15, 1817, was indentured with the consent of his mother (not named) to George W. Bradford in 1817 to learn to be a farmer.

NEEL, JOHN, master of Susanna Patrick and Ann Patrick in 1804 indentures.

NELLEY (Negro), mother of Negro Hosea, an illegitimate child (born in 1810), in 1811 indenture.

NELSON, AQUILA, guardian of Bennett Vansickle in 1802.

NELSON, JAMES, guardian of Penelope Rutledge, Thomas Rutledge, and Jacob Rutledge in 1826.

NEVIL, MARY ("a yellow girl"), age 3 years and 6 months in March, 1807, was indentured to Benjamin Richardson in 1807 to learn to do housework.

NEVILL, PHEBE, age 11 on June 13, 1824, was indentured with the consent of the Trustee of the Poor to William Bay in 1824 to learn to do housework and be a servant.

NEVILL, PHOEBE, age 5 on June 30, 1819, was indentured with the consent of her mother (not named) to Samuel F. Rigdon in 1820 to learn to do housework.

NEVILL, SIMON, master of Negro Rachel in 1815 indenture.

NEVILL, WILLIAM, master of Thomas Montgomery (son of Thomas Montgomery) in 1816 indenture.

NINDE, BENJAMIN (son of James Ninde, Sr.), age 16 on January 13, 1805, was indentured to John S. Peck & Company in 1805 to learn to be a tanner.

NINDE, JAMES SR., father of Benjamin Ninde in 1805 indenture.

NORRINGTON, ELIAS (son of Sarah Norrington), age 4 on October 30, 1808, was indentured to James Alexander in 1808 to learn to be a farmer.

NORRINGTON, ELIAS, age 8 on October 30, 1814, was indentured with the consent of his mother (not named) to John Porter in 1815 to learn to be a weaver.

NORRINGTON, GRAFTON ROBINSON (son of Sarah Norrington), age 4 on June 26, 1804, was indentured to Evan Evans in 1804 to learn to be a wheelwright.

NORRINGTON, JAMES (son of Sarah Norrington), age 14 on October 20, 1821, was indentured to Edward Judd in 1821 to learn to be a shoemaker.

NORRINGTON, MARY (daughter of Sarah Norrington), age 7 on March

10, 1804, was indentured to Hugh Bay in 1804 to learn to do housework.

NORRINGTON, MARY ANN, age 6 on February 18, 1814, was indentured to Isaac Pyle in 1814 to learn to do housework.

NORRINGTON, SARAH, mother of Mary Norrington and Grafton Robinson Norrington in 1804 indentures, Elias Norrington in 1808 indenture, and James Norrington in 1821 indenture.

NORRIS, AQUILA, master of John Dutton in 1805 indenture.

NORRIS, CATHARINE, wife of Daniel Norris in 1802 indenture.

NORRIS, DANIEL AND CATHARINE (his wife), masters of Charity Chance (Mulatto) in 1802 indenture.

NORRIS, DAVID (son of Jesse Norris), no age given in July, 1819, was indentured to Daniel Lamborn in 1820 to learn to be a paper maker.

NORRIS, EDWARD, father of John Norris in 1816 indenture record.

NORRIS, EDWARD, master of Samuel Garrett (Negro) in 1822 indenture.

NORRIS, JACOB, age 13 on April 1, 1809, was indentured with the consent of his mother (not named) to Claudius Standiford in 1809 to learn to be a taylor.

NORRIS, JAMES (illegitimate child), age 8 on January 24, 1822, was indentured to Jeremiah Bennington in 1822 to learn to be a farmer.

NORRIS, JAMES (son of Jesse Norris), no age given in February, 1815, was indentured to Morris Maulsby to learn to be a blacksmith.

NORRIS, JESSE, father of James Norris in 1815 indenture.

NORRIS, JESSE, father of David Norris in 1820 indenture.

NORRIS, JOHN (son of Edward Norris), master of Negro William in 1816 indenture.

NORRIS, JOHN, master of Henry Smith (son of Grace Smith) in 1818 indenture.

NORRIS, RHESA, guardian of John Gallion, William Gallion, and Hannah Gallion in 1818.

NORRIS, WILLIAM, age 15 years and 6 months in April, 1809, was indentured with the consent of his mother (not named) to Aquila McComas in 1809 to learn to be a blacksmith.

NOWLAND, EBENEZER. age 13 on May 13, 1801, was indentured to Joshua Wood in 1801 to learn to be a hat maker.

NOWREY, NANCY (illegitimate child), age 4 in August, 1805, was indentured to John Hanway in 1806 to learn to do housework.

NOWREY, NANCY, age 6 in 1807, was indentured to James Amos in November, 1807.

NUMBERS, JAMES (orphan), age 15 on May 24, 1811, was indentured to Nathan Grafton in 1812 to learn to be a boot maker.

O'BRIAN, JOHN (of Baltimore County), guardian of Eleanor O'Neal and Barnard O'Neil in 1806.

O'DANEL, JOHN, master of Edmond Bull (son of Sarah Bull) in 1807 indenture.

O'NEAL, BARNARD, age 14 in April 15, 1812. Court appointed John Reardon as his guardian in 1812.

O'NEAL, ELEANOR, age 9 in January, 1806. Court appointed John O'Brian, of Baltimore County, as her guardian in 1806.

O'NEAL, ELEANOR, age 15 on January 10, 1812. Court appointed John Reardon as her guardian in 1812.

O'NEAL, HENRY, master of Emanuel Fox (Negro) in 1828 indenture.

O'NEIL, BARNARD, age 8 in 1806. Court appointed John O'Brian, of Baltimore County, as his guardian in 1806.

O'NEIL, HENRY, master of Mary Jay (Negro) in 1829 indenture.

O'NEIL, JOHN, master of Isaiah Wilson (Negro) in 1828 indenture.

O'NEILL, JOHN, master of Thomas Haskell and David Boyles in 1820 indentures.

OLIVER, BENNETT, age 8 on February 28, 1815, was indentured with the consent of his mother (not named) to Frances E. Monks in 1815 to learn to be a farmer.

OLIVER, HENRY (illegitimate child), age 7 on October 17, 1818, was indentured with the consent of his mother (not named) to John Daugherty in 1819 to learn to be a farmer.

ONION, CORBIN L., guardian of Susannah Gough in 1811.

ONION, CORBIN LEE, guardian of Prudence Gough in 1810.

ORR, JAMES, master of Elisha Parr and Jacob Stricklen in 1807 indentures.

ORR, JAMES, master of John P. Bradford (Negro) in 1829 indenture.

ORR, JAMES, master of George Swarth (son of Samuel Swarth) in 1812 indenture.

ORR, JAMES, master of John Stricklen (orphan) and Theodocey Stricklen (orphan) in 1810 indentures.

OSBORN, GEORGE, master of Jack Robinson (Negro) in 1822 indenture.

OSBORN, JAMES (son of William Osborn), age 18 on February 8, 1806. Court appointed John Courtney as his guardian in 1806.

OSBORN, THEADORE, no age given in 1827. Court appointed William Bradford as his guardian on March 20, 1827.

OSBORN, WILLIAM, father of James Osborn in 1806 guardianship.

OSBORN, WILLIAM, no age given in 1827. Court appointed William Bradford as his guardian on March 20, 1827.

OSBORN [OSBERN?], WILLIAM (orphan), age 14 on December 4, 1825, was indentured "with the consent of his friends" to William Bradford in 1826 to learn to be a hatter.

PACA, JAMES, master of George Baker (son of Gideon Baker) in 1811 indenture.

PACA, JAMES, master of John B. Roberts in 1813 indenture.

PACA, WILLIAM (orphan), age 15 on May 11, 1827, was indentured with the consent of his mother (not named) to William McComas in 1828 to learn to be a carpenter.

PACA, WILLIAM, no age given in 1804. Court appointed Richard E. Dallam as his guardian in 1804.

PACKWOOD, JAMES (orphan), age 16 on May 14, 1808, was indentured to James Taylor in 1808 to learn to be a blacksmith.

PANNELL, JAMES, guardian of Deliverance H. Glasgow, James Glasgow, and George R. Glasgow, and administrator of Elizh[?] Glasgow in 1830.

PARKER, SAMUEL G., master of Ann Maria Gibson (daughter of Hannah Gibson) in 1819 indenture.

PARR, ELISHA, age 15 on August 27, 1807, was indentured to James Orr in 1807 to learn to be a potter.

PARSONS, ABRAHAM, no age given in 1816, was indentured with the consent of his parents (not named) to Morris Maulsby in 1816 to learn to be a blacksmith.

PARSONS, CALEB (a free Negro son of Moses Parsons), age 11 on

August 20, 1807, was indentured to Christian Waskey in 1807 to learn to be a shoemaker.

PARSONS, HIRAM, "orphan sent to this county [Harford] from the Alms House in Baltimore," age 13 on March 3, 1830, was indentured to John Rogers in 1830 to learn to be a farmer.

PARSONS, JOHN (son of John Parsons), no age given in 1806, was indentured with the consent of his father to John Rouse in 1806 to learn to be a spinning wheel maker.

PARSONS, JOHN, father of John Parsons in 1806 indenture.

PARSONS, JOSEPH D., master of James Thrift (alias Taylor) in 1816 indenture.

PARSONS, MOSES (Negro), father of Caleb Parsons in 1807 indenture.

PASSEY [TASSEY?], WILLIAM, no age given in 1820, was indentured with the consent of his father (not named) to Joseph Whitson to learn to be a blacksmith.

PATRICK, ANN (daughter of Ruth Patrick), age 2 in June, 1803, was indentured to John Neal in 1804 to learn to do housework.

PATRICK, GEORGE (son of Ruth Patrick), age 7 in January, 1804, was indentured to Henry Fullard to learn to be a farmer.

PATRICK, RUTH, mother of George Patrick, Susanna Patrick, Ann Patrick, and Sarah Patrick in 1804 indentures.

PATRICK, SARAH (daughter of Ruth Patrick), age 13 in January, 1804, was indentured to Thomas Sheridine in 1804 to learn to do housework.

PATRICK, SUSANNA (daughter of Ruth Patrick), age 9 in March, 1804, was indentured to John Neal in 1804 to learn to do housework.

PATTERSON, ROBERT, master of John Adams (orphan) in 1826 indenture.

PATTY (Negro), "a yellow child," age 6 in October, 1817, was indentured to Frances Maulsby in 1818 to learn to do housework.

PAYNE, BENJAMIN, age 17 in December, 1823. Court appointed Charlotte Payne as his guardian in 1824.

PAYNE, BENJAMIN, deceased by 1823, husband of Charlotte Payne.

PAYNE, CHARLOTTE (widow of Benjamin Payne), guardian of Benjamin Payne and Josias Payne in 1824.

PAYNE, JOSIAS, age 8 in May, 1824. Court appointed Charlotte Payne as his guardian in 1824.

PEARCE, EDWARD, guardian of Elisha Hall and Ann Hall in 1806.

PEARSON, RACHEL, master of Negro Evelina (illegitimate) in 1815 indenture.

PECK, ELIZA JANE (Negro orphan), age 5 on April 1, 1829, was indentured to Mortimore Cunningham in 1829 to learn to be a servant.

PECK, JOHN S., master of James Armont in 1806 indenture.

PECK, JOHN SPOTSWOOD AND COMPANY, master of Benjamin Ninde, James Spence, and James Keys in 1805, and James Armont in 1806.

PECK, JOHN SPOTSWOOD, master of Luda Thomas (Negro) in 1803 indenture.

PECK, JOHN SPOTSWOOD, master of Elizabeth Talbott (Negro) in 1806 indenture.

PEERCE, STEPHEN A., master of Robert Johnson, Septimus Presbury, and Thomas Leastater in 1826 indentures.

PENIX, EDWARD (son of John Penix), age 16 on August 2, 1804, was
    indentured to William Silver in 1804 to learn to be a hatter.
PENIX, JAMES, master of William Pennix [sic] in 1802 indenture.
PENIX, JOHN, father of Edward Penix in 1804 indenture.
PENNINGTON, ISAAC, master of Lewis Ponian (Mulatto) in 1815
    indenture.
PENNIX, JOHN, father of William Pennix in 1802 indenture.
PENNIX, WILLIAM, no age given in 1802, was indentured with the
    consent of his father, John Pennix, to James Penix [sic] in
    1802 to learn to be a tanner and currier.
PERINE, ANN, age 8 in 1801. Court appointed William and Jane
    Grafton as her guardian in 1801.
PERINE, MARTHA, age 13 in 1801. Court appointed Hannah Armstrong
    as her guardian in 1801.
PERINE, NIMROD, age 10 in 1801. Court appointed Hannah Armstrong
    as his guardian in 1801.
PERRY, JAMES (orphan), age 16 on August 15, 1806, was indentured
    to Benjamin Jervis in 1806 to learn to be a cooper.
PERRYMAN, ISAAC, master of James How (orphan) in 1814 indenture.
PETERS, JOHN WASHINGTON, age 9 in March, 1828, was indentured to
    William Michael in 1828 to learn to be a farmer.
PHEBE (Negro), mother of Negro Priss in 1804 indenture.
PHILIP (Negro), age about 27, valued at $300, and formerly owned
    by William Calwell, deceased, in October, 1823.
PHILLIPS, JAMES, deceased father of James Martha Phillips in
    1812.
PHILLIPS, JAMES MARTHA, daughter of Sarah Phillips (widow of
    James Phillips), age 2 on September 29, 1811. Court appointed
    Paca Smith as her guardian in 1812.
PHILLIPS, SARAH, mother of James Martha Phillips in 1812 record.
PIERCE, STEPHEN A., master of James Sewell in 1827 indenture.
PIERCE, WILLIAM H., master of James Johnson, George Johnson, and
    John Richards in 1822 indentures.
PIERCE, WILLIAM, master of James Henry Simmons in 1823 indenture.
PINNION, WILLIAM, "abandoned by his parents," age 7 in February,
    1815, was indentured to Howes Goldsborough in 1815 to learn to
    be a waiter or house servant.
POGUE, JOHN, master of Charles Herren (illegitimate child) in
    1808 indenture.
POLSON, ELIAS ("a free Mulatto"), age 14 years and 6 months in
    May, 1803, was indentured to William Robinson in 1803 to learn
    to be a cooper.
PONIAN, LEWIS (Mulatto), age 12 in October, 1815, was indentured
    to Isaac Pennington in 1815 to learn to be a flour barrel
    maker.
PORTER, JOHN, master of Elias Norrington in 1815 indenture.
POTEET, CHINWORTH, age 11 on September 9, 1813. Court appointed
    Jesse Poteet as his guardian in 1814.
POTEET, JESSE, guardian of Chinworth Poteet in 1814.
PRESBURY, EDWARD (Negro son of Tamer Presbury), age 6 on
    September 1, 1804, was indentured to Dr. Wakeman Bryerly in
    1805 to learn to be a farmer.
PRESBURY, EDWARD, age 18 in May, 1826. Court appointed John B.
    Bayless as his guardian on January 9, 1827.
PRESBURY, ELLEN, age 12 in February, 1826. Court appointed John

B. Bayless as her guardian on January 9, 1827.

PRESBURY, GEORGE G. (of Baltimore City), master of Elizabeth Monahan in 1810 indenture.

PRESBURY, GEORGE G. (of Baltimore City), master of Thomas C.[G?] Howard in 1812 indenture.

PRESBURY, JAMES L., age about 12 in 1828. Court appointed Thomas Dorney as his guardian on December 8, 1828.

PRESBURY, OCTAVIUS, age 12 in September, 1826. Court appointed John B. Bayless as his guardian on January 9, 1827.

PRESBURY, SEPTIMUS (orphan), age 16 on November 15, 1825, was indentured "with the consent of his friends" to Stephen A. Peerce in 1826 to learn to be a hatter.

PRESBURY, SEPTIMUS, age 17 in October, 1826. Court appointed John B. Bayless as his guardian on January 9, 1827.

PRESBURY, SOPHIA, age 15 in August, 1826. Court appointed John B. Bayless as her guardian on January 9, 1827.

PRESBURY, TAMER (Negro), father of Edward Presbury in 1805 record.

PRESBURY, WILLIAM, no age given in March, 1817, was indentured with the consent of his father (not named) to George Griffith in 1817 to learn to be a farmer.

PRESTON, BARNARD, liberated Hanna Preston (Negro) prior to 1814.

PRESTON, BILL (Negro), son of Hannah Preston, age 8 on July 26, 1814, was indentured to William Hanna in 1814 to learn to be a farmer.

PRESTON, GIDEON VANCLAVE, age 16 in June, 1802. Court appointed his mother, Mary Preston, as his guardian in 1802.

PRESTON, HANNA (Negro liberated by Barnard Preston), mother of Bill Preston in 1814 indenture.

PRESTON, JAMES BARNET, age 12 on November 13, 1801. Court appointed his mother, Mary Preston, as his guardian in 1802.

PRESTON, JAMES BOND, guardian of James M. Wilmer in 1812.

PRESTON, MARY, mother and guardian of Gideon Vanclave Preston, Sarah Ruff Preston, and James Barnet Preston in 1802 guardianships.

PRESTON, NAT (Negro), son of Sam Preston, age 11 years and 17 days on February 26, 1811, was indentured to John Jewett in 1811 to learn to be a farmer.

PRESTON, SAM ("a free Negro"), father of Nat Preston in 1811 indenture.

PRESTON, SARAH RUFF, age 14 in June, 1802. Court appointed her mother, Mary Preston, as her guardian in 1802.

PREWETT, ROBERT (illegitimate child), age 14 on November 22, 1820, was indentured with the consent of his mother (not named) to Joseph Whitson in 1821 to learn to be a blacksmith.

PRICE AND STUMP, millers and masters of Jesse Davis in 1805 indenture.

PRICE, DAVID E., master of Jacob Watters in 1806 indenture.

PRICE, JAMES (orphan), age 17 on January 17, 1817, was indentured to James H. Foard in 1817 to learn to be a cooper.

PRICE, JOHN HENRY, age 4 on June 8, 1812. Court appointed John Stump (son of Henry Stump) as his guardian with the consent of his mother (not named) in 1812.

PRICE, JOHN, master of Benjamin Curry (son of John Curry) in 1816 indenture.

PRICE, JOSEPH (son of Robert Price), age 16 on June 17, 1807, was
indentured to Abner Gilbert in 1808 to learn to be a carpenter
and house joiner.

PRICE, MARGARET ANN, age 1 on April 18, 1812. Court appointed
John Stump (son of Henry Stump) as her guardian with the
consent of her mother (not named) in 1812.

PRICE, RACHEL, age 2 on December 9, 1811. Court appointed John
Stump (son of Henry Stump) as her guardian with the consent of
her mother (not named) in 1812.

PRICE, ROBERT, father of Joseph Price in 1808 indenture.

PRICE, STEPHEN A., see "Stephen A. Peerce," q.v., in 1826.

PRICE, STEPHEN A., master of James Griffith in 1825 indenture.

PRICE, WILLIAM and wife (not named), masters of Negro Fanny in
1811 indenture.

PRICE, WILLIAM, master of Negro Lee (illegitimate child) in 1813
indenture.

PRIGG, CUBIT (Negro, son of Jenny Prigg), age 6 in April, 1827,
was indentured with the consent of his mother to Daniel Bay in
1828 to learn to be a distiller.

PRIGG, EDWARD, by his 1826 will, freed Minty Prigg (Negro) and
Julian Prigg (Negro) in December, 1826 [1828?].

PRIGG, JENNY, mother of Cubit Prigg (Negro) in 1828 indenture.

PRIGG, JULIAN (Negro), age about 18 in 1826, by the will of
Edward Prigg in 1826, was freed on December 11, 1826 [1828?].

PRIGG, MINTY (Negro), age about 16 in 1826, by the will of Edward
Prigg in 1826, was freed on December 11, 1826 [1828?].

PRINE, AMOS (illegitimate), age 15 on August 4, 1828, was
indentured to William Amoss in 1828 to learn to be a
blacksmith.

PRINGLE, MARK (Baltimore merchant), master of James Giles in 1807
indenture.

PRISS (Negro daughter of Negro Phebe), age 6 on October 4, 1803,
was indentured to Samuel Bradford in 1804 to learn to do
housework.

PRISS (Negro), mother of Negro Fanny in 1804 indenture.

PRITCHARD, ASAEL, age 17 on November 16, 1812, was indentured
with the consent of his mother (not named) to Abraham Gorrell
in 1813 to learn to be a house carpenter.

PRITCHARD, SAMUEL, age 13 in 1802, was indentured to William
Arnold in 1802 to learn to be a tanner and currier.

PROCTOR, THOMAS, master of Benjamin McCullough (son of Robert
McCullough) in 1806 indenture.

PROVY (Negro), "a yellow girl," age 4 in August, 1821, was
indentured to Benjamin Richardson in 1821 to learn to do
housework.

PYLE, ISAAC, master of Mary Ann Norrington in 1814 indenture.

PYLE, WILLIAM, guardian of James Thomas, Hannah Thomas, John
Thomas and William Thomas (children of John and Mary Thomas)
in 1806.

QUARLES, ELIZABETH, master of Myrtilla Husband (Negro) in 1811
indenture.

QUARLL, WILLIAM, master of Susanna Lynum or Linom (daughter of
Ann Lynum or Linom) in 1802 indenture.

QUINLAN, CHARITY, age 7 on May 8, 1823. Court appointed Samuel
Macatee as her guardian in 1823.

QUINLAN, CHARLES, age 5 on November 18, 1822. Court appointed
Samuel Macatee as his guardian in 1823.

QUINLAN, LUCINDA (orphan), age 7 on July 22, 1830, was indentured
to Ann Daugherty in 1830 to learn "all branches of housework."

QUINLAN, PHILIP THOMAS, age 9 on July 25, 1823. Court appointed
Samuel Macatee as his guardian in 1823.

QUINLAN, RACHEL ANN, age 11 on July 11, 1823. Court appointed
Samuel Macatee as her guardian in 1823.

QULLUM [?], RICHARD, master of Negro George in 1821 indenture.

RACHEL (Negro, daughter of Negro Fanny), age 10 in 1803, was
indentured to John Rouse in 1803 to learn to do housework.

RACHEL (Negro orphan), age 6 on January 1, 1816, was indentured
to Simon Nevill in 1815 to learn to do housework.

RACHEL (Negro), mother of Negro Solomon in 1803 indenture.

RAGAN, DANIEL (orphan), age 8 on November 28, 1808, was
indentured to John Daugherty in 1809 to learn to be a farmer.

REA, SAMUEL, former guardian of William Barnes prior to 1806 when
he (Rea) reportedly "has left this state."

REARDON, JOHN, guardian of Bernard O'Neal and Eleanor O'Neal in
1812.

REARDON, PATRICK, master of John Lawrence in 1802 indenture.

REED AND DAVIS (Upton Reed and Rees Davis, cutlers), masters of
Daniel Jackson in 1810, James Morford in 1812, and Ephraim
Swart in 1813.

REED, UPTON, see "Reed and Davis," q.v.

RENSHAW, ELIZABETH, wife of John Renshaw in 1808 indenture.

RENSHAW, JOHN AND ELIZABETH, masters of Susannah Wilgis in 1808
indenture.

RENSHAW, NAOMI, natural guardian of James Calder and Lloyd Calder
in 1817.

REYNOLDS, JESSE, guardian of Absalom Brown, Josiah Brown, Elwood
Brown, and Rachel Brown in 1822.

RHODA (Negro), age 6 in January, 1827, was indentured with the
consent of her mother (not named) to John Brannon in 1827 to
learn to do housework.

RHODES, ELI (son of Hannah Rhodes), age illegible, was indentured
to John Levin [Lewin?] in 1801 to learn to be a chair maker.

RHODES, HANNAH, age illegible, was indentured to Henrietta
Wheeler in 1801 [Record illegible; probably daughter of Hannah
Rhodes].

RHODES, HANNAH, mother of Eli Rhodes in 1801 indenture.

RICHARD (Negro son of Negro Margaret), no age given in 1803, was
indentured to Henry G. Bussey in 1803 to learn to be a farmer.

RICHARDS, JOHN (orphan), age 19 on May 20, 1822, was indentured
to William H. Pierce in 1822 to learn to be a hatter.

RICHARDSON, BENJAMIN (son of Samuel Richardson), guardian of
William Sharp, Elizabeth Sharp, and Susan Sharp in 1803.

RICHARDSON, BENJAMIN, father of Martin Richardson in 1822
indenture.

RICHARDSON, BENJAMIN, master of Mary Nevil ("a yellow girl") in
1807 indenture.

RICHARDSON, BENJAMIN, master of Negro Provy ("a yellow girl") in
1821 indenture.

RICHARDSON, MARTIN (son of Benjamin Richardson), no age given in
September, 1822, was indentured with the consent of his father

to Washington Hanway in 1822 to learn "wooling manufactory."
RICHARDSON, SAMUEL, age 12 in October, 1818. Court appointed
    William Amoss as his guardian in 1819.
RICHARDSON, SAMUEL, father of Benjamin Richardson in 1803 record.
RICHARDSON, SAMUEL, master of Joshua J.[?] Bond in 1816
    indenture.
RICHARDSON, SPENCER (Negro), by the will of James Garrettson in
    1805, was freed on January 26, 1828.
RICHARDSON, THOMAS, age 15 on January 10, 1819. Court appointed
    William Amoss as his guardian in 1819.
RICHARDSON, WILLIAM, master of Moses Martin (Negro) in 1813
    indenture.
RICHARDSON, WILLIAM, master of Negro William in 1816 indenture.
RICHARDSON, WILLIAM SR., master of John Brewer in 1821 indenture.
RICKETS, THOMAS, master of Thomas Waltham (illegitimate son of
    Hannah Johnston) in 1823 indenture.
RICKETTS, SAMUEL, father of William Ricketts in 1820 indenture.
RICKETTS, SAMUEL, master of Negro William in 1811 indenture.
RICKETTS, WILLIAM (son of Samuel Ricketts), no age given in June,
    1820, was indentured to William Bradford to learn to be a
    hatter.
RIGBY, WILLIAM (Negro, son of William Rigby), age 8 on August 1,
    1829, was indentured to Thomas C. Stump in 1829 to learn to be
    a farmer.
RIGBY, WILLIAM (Negro), father of William Rigby in 1829
    indenture.
RIGDON, SAMUEL F., master of Phoebe Nevill in 1820 indenture.
RILEY, LLOYD (illegitimate child), age 10 on April 7, 1827, was
    indentured with the consent of his mother (not named) to
    William McComas in 1828 to learn to be a carpenter.
ROBERTS, ISAIAH AND MARY, masters of Negro Amea in 1812
    indenture.
ROBERTS, JOHN B., age 11 on February 21, 1814, was indentured
    with the consent of his father (not named) to James Paca in
    1813 to learn to be a shoemaker.
ROBERTS, JOHN, guardian of Cordelia Debrular in 1802.
ROBERTS, JOHN, master of Daniel York (orphan) in 1808 indenture.
ROBERTS, MARY AND ISAIAH, masters of Negro Amea in 1812
    indenture.
ROBINSON, GEORGE, master of Herman Creige (orphan) in 1806
    indenture.
ROBINSON, JACK (Negro), age 15 in October, 1821, was indentured
    to George Osborn in 1822 to learn to be a farmer.
ROBINSON, JOHN (son of Joseph Robinson), no age given in August,
    1804, was indentured to Joseph Stokes in 1804 to learn to be a
    house carpenter.
ROBINSON, JOSEPH, father of John Robinson in 1804 indenture.
ROBINSON, JOSEPH, guardian of William Ward, James Ward, and
    Richard Ward in 1802.
ROBINSON, JOSEPH, master of Negro Abraham in 1808 indenture.
ROBINSON, WILLIAM, master of Elias Polson (free Mulatto) and
    William Twogood [Toogood] in 1803 indentures.
ROGERS, JANE, wife of Rolen Rogers in 1801 indenture.
ROGERS, JOHN, master of Hiram Parsons in 1830 indenture.
ROGERS, ROLEN AND JANE (his wife), masters of Elizabeth Thompson

in 1801 indenture.

ROSS, ASABELLE [ARABELLE?], mother of David Ross in 1815 indenture.

ROSS, DAVID, "his father away as a soldier and his mother Asabelle [Arabelle?] unable to support him," age 14 in July, 1815, was indentured to John Wood (son of James Wood), of Havre de Grace, Maryland, to learn to be a taylor.

ROUSE, JOHN and wife (not named), masters of Hetty Giberson in 1802 indenture.

ROUSE, JOHN, master of John Harkins (son of Aaron Harkins) in 1802 indenture.

ROUSE, JOHN, master of Negro Frances (daughter of Negro Hetty) in 1810 indenture.

ROUSE, JOHN, master of Ambrose Lytle (orphan) in 1828 indenture.

ROUSE, JOHN, master of John Morford in 1807 indenture.

ROUSE, JOHN, master of John Parsons (son of John Parsons) in 1806 indenture.

ROUSE, JOHN, master of Negro Rachel (daughter of Negro Fanny) in 1803 indenture.

ROW, CORNROD [CONRAD?], father of Samuel Row in 1805 indenture.

ROW, SAMUEL (son of Cornrod Row), no age given in June, 1805, was indentured to John Smith in 1805 to learn to be a tanner.

RUFF, GEORGE (Negro), by the will of Ruth Wilmott in 1812, was freed on April 20, 1824, and it was acknowledged in Court on June 3, 1828.

RUFF, HENRY, age 14 on May 4, 1810. Court appointed William Bull as his guardian in 1810.

RUFF, HENRY, age 11 on May 4, 1806. Court appointed John Ruff as his guardian in 1807.

RUFF, JOHN, guardian of Richard Ruff and Henry Ruff in 1807.

RUFF, RICHARD, age 19 on January 30, 1810. Court appointed William Bull as his guardian in 1810.

RUFF, RICHARD, age 16 on January 30, 1807. Court appointed John Ruff as his guardian in 1807.

RUMSEY, CHARLES HENRY, age 11 in August, 1807. Court appointed Henry Rumsey (of New York) as his guardian in 1808.

RUMSEY, HENRY (of New York), guardian of Charles Henry Rumsey in 1808.

RUMSEY, JOHN, guardian of William Hall and Nathan Hall in 1804.

RUSSELL, ALISANNA, mother of Abraham Ditto (an orphan boy) in 1806.

RUTH, JANE, mother of Hugh Gladden (illegitimate child) in 1808 indenture.

RUTH, PARKER (illegitimate child), age 17 on December 14, 1808, was indentured with the consent of his mother (not named) to William Kithcart in 1808 to learn to be a farmer.

RUTLEDGE, ABRAHAM, master of Isaac Johnson (Negro) in 1830 indenture.

RUTLEDGE, JACOB, no age given in 1826. Court appointed James Nelson as his guardian in April, 1826.

RUTLEDGE, JOSHUA, master of Joshua Scott in 1826 indenture.

RUTLEDGE, PENELOPE, no age given in 1826. Court appointed James Nelson as her guardian in April, 1826.

RUTLEDGE, THOMAS, no age given in 1826. Court appointed James Nelson as his guardian in April, 1826.

SAM (Negro orphan), age 11 on December 25, 1820, was indentured to William Divers in 1820 to learn to be a cooper.

SAMPSON, THOMAS, master of Benjamin Brusebanks (orphan) in 1806 indenture.

SAMPSON, THOMAS, master of John Andrews in 1802 indenture.

SANDERS, ARAMENTA, age about 8 in May, 1824. Court appointed John Sanders as her guardian in 1825.

SANDERS, JOHN, guardian of Aramenta Sanders in 1824.

SANDERS, ROBERT B., age 6 on March 29, 1813, was indentured with the consent of his grandmother (not named) to Elijah Waskey in 1813 to learn to be a boot and shoemaker.

SANTEE, GEORGE W. (son of Honora Santee), age 15 on January 4, 1817, was indentured to Bennett Taylor in 1816 to learn to be a taylor.

SANTEE, HONORA, mother of George W. Santee in 1816 indenture.

SARAH (Negro, "born free of Negro Jane who was set free by Joseph Miller, deceased"), age 5 years and 3 months as of February 7, 1806, was indentured to Edward Miller in 1806 to learn to do housework.

SARAH (Negro), "a poor girl," age 5 on August 1, 1829, was indentured to David Swart in 1829 to learn to be a housekeeper.

SARAH (Negro), age 9 on May 1, 1816, was indentured with the consent of her mother (not named) to George W. Bradford in 1817 to learn to be a servant.

SARAH (Negro), age about 8 in 1823, valued at $80, and formerly owned by William Calwell, deceased, in October, 1823.

SARAH (Negro), mother of Negro Lewis amd Negro Charles in 1817 indentures.

SARAH ELIZABETH JANE (Colored orphan), age 10 in December, 1825, was indentured to Mary Wilson in 1826 to learn to do housework.

SARRAH, ELIZABETH (illegitimate child), age 18 months in June, 1823, was indentured with the consent of her mother (not named) to John Dallam in 1823.

SAUNDERS, EDWARD, age 17 on March 31, 1814, was indentured with the consent of his mother (not named) to John Anderson in 1814 to learn to be a cooper.

SAUNDERS, WILLIAM, age 11 on March 14, 1814, was indentured with the consent of his mother (not named) to John Anderson in 1814 to learn to be a cooper.

SCARBOROUGH, EANUS (orphan), age 17 on June 15, 1816, was indentured to Samuel Ailes in 1817 to learn to be a mason.

SCARBOROUGH, EUCLIDUS, master of Negro Harriot in 1811 indenture.

SCARBOROUGH, JOHN, master of Elizabeth Evatt (daughter of Richard Evatt) in 1809 indenture.

SCARBOROUGH, JOSEPH, father of Samuel Scarborough in 1801 indenture.

SCARBOROUGH, SAMUEL (son of Joseph Scarborough), age 16 on May 25, 1800, was indentured to Benjamin Duberry in 1801 "to learn his trade" [not specified in the record].

SCARFF, HENRY, guardian of Susan Thompson and John Thompson in 1818.

SCOTT, JOSHUA (illegitimate child), age 5 on January 1, 1826, was indentured with the consent of his mother (not named) to

Joshua Rutledge in 1826 to learn to be a farmer.

SCOTT, SARAH YORK, age 12 on May 8, 1803. Court appointed Zelfa York as her guardian in 1803.

SCOTT, THOMAS, master of Mary Ann Bodden in 1820 indenture.

SEARS, MARY (Mrs.), of Havre de Grace, Maryland, master of Harriot (Mulatto orphan) and Negro Eliza in 1815 indentures.

SENY [?], SAMUEL (Negro orphan), age 17 on December 25, 1805, was indentured to Richard Coale in 1806 to learn to be a farmer.

SEWELL, JAMES, age 14 on March 15, 1826, was indentured "with the consent of his friends" to Stephen A. Pierce in 1827 to learn to be a hatter.

SHACKELL, MARY, guardian of Emarrilla Spencer in 1819.

SHARLOTTE (Negro), age 5 on October 15, 1808, was indentured to David Tate in 1808.

SHARP, ELIZABETH, age 15 in April, 1803. Court appointed Benjamin Richardson (son of Samuel Richardson) as her guardian in 1803.

SHARP, SUSAN, age 12 in August, 1803. Court appointed Benjamin Richardson (son of Samuel Richardson) as her guardian in 1803.

SHARP, WILLIAM, age 14 on October 15, 1802. Court appointed Benjamin Richardson (son of Samuel Richardson) as his guardian in 1803.

SHAY, BENNET (illegitimate child), age 14 on March 2, 1821, was indentured with the consent of his mother (not named) to John Gray in 1821 to learn to be a shoemaker.

SHAY, CLARISSA AND THOMAS, masters of Negro Adeline in 1812 indenture.

SHAY, THOMAS, master of Mulatto Aquila and Negro Adeline in 1812 indentures.

SHAY, THOMAS, master of Negro boy Michael and Negro boy Henry in 1814, "but he (Shay) lately died [in 1822], leaving no widow," so these boys were indentured to Jason Moore to learn to be farmers in May, 1822.

SHAY, THOMAS, master of Negro Harry and Negro Mike in 1813 indentures.

SHERIDINE, RUTHA, master of Margaret Fisher (orphan) in 1818 indenture.

SHERIDINE, THOMAS, master of Sarah Patrick in 1804 indenture.

SHEWELL, THOMAS, age 15 on April 9, 1811, was indentured with the consent of his mother (not named) to William Careins in 1811 to learn to be a spinning wheel maker.

SHOADY, JAMES, age 14 on February 2, 1802, was indentured to James Taylor in 1801 to learn to be a farmer.

SILLOCK, BENJAMIN, age 1 in October, 1822. Court appointed Hannah Sillock as his guardian in 1823, with Hanford Sillock and Nathaniel Sillock as securities.

SILLOCK, CATY ANN, age 13 in February, 1823. Court appointed Hannah Sillock as her guardian in 1823, with Hanford Sillock and Nathaniel Sillock as securities.

SILLOCK, HANFORD, security for Hannah Sillock in 1823 guardianship.

SILLOCK, HANNAH, guardian of Caty Ann Sillock and Benjamin Sillock in 1823.

SILLOCK, NATHANIEL, security for Hannah Sillock in 1823 guardianship.

SILVER, WILLIAM, master of Edward Penix (son of John Penix) in

1804 indenture.

SIMMONS, JAMES HENRY (son of William Simmons), age 10 on May 16, 1822, was indentured with the consent of his father to William Pierce in 1823 to learn to be a hatter.

SIMMONS, WILLIAM, father of James Henry Simmons in 1823 indenture.

SIMS, WILLIAM, master of William Ward (orphan) in 1802 indenture.

SINCLAIR, TEMPERANCE, mother of Anne West in 1806 indenture.

SINGLETON, GEORGE, age 13 on February 15, 1820, was indentured with the consent of his mother (not named) to William Heaps in 1820 to learn to be a farmer and shoemaker.

SINGLETON, HENRY, age 10 on July 9, 1821, was indentured with the consent of his mother (not named) to Nathaniel Brindley in 1822 to learn to be a shoemaker.

SINGLETON, JOHN, father of William Singleton in 1813 indenture.

SINGLETON, JOHN, father of Phebe Singleton in 1809 indenture.

SINGLETON, PHEBE (daughter of John Singleton), age 7 on December 9, 1808, was indentured to James Kerr in 1809 to learn to do housework.

SINGLETON, RICHARD, age 8 years and 6 months on May 10, 1821, was indentured with the consent of his mother (not named) to John Heaton in 1822 to learn to be a house carpenter.

SINGLETON, WILLIAM (son of John Singleton), age 13 on February 7, 1813, was indentured to William Adams in 1813 to learn to be a stone mason.

SLADE, ELIZABETH, "youngest unmarried daughter of William Slade, deceased," in May, 1824, no age given.

SLADE, WILLIAM, deceased father of Elizabeth Slade in 1824.

SMITH, BETSY, age 14 on November 26, 1805. Court appointed Frances Smith as her guardian in 1806.

SMITH, FRANCES, guardian of Betsy Smith, James G. Smith, and John Smith in 1806.

SMITH, FREENETTA, age 4 on November 10, 1801. Court appointed her mother, Martha Smith, as her guardian in 1802.

SMITH, GEORGE, master of John Forwood (son of Elizabeth Forwood) in 1805 indenture.

SMITH, GRACE, mother of Henry Smith in 1818 indenture.

SMITH, HENRY (son of Grace Smith), age 11 on April 9, 1817, was indentured to John Norris in 1818 to learn to be a farmer.

SMITH, HENRY, master of William Henry Bradford (Negro) in 1828.

SMITH, ISAAC, master of Daniel McKan (McKam?) in 1810 indenture.

SMITH, JAMES G., age 12 on November 25, 1805. Court appointed Frances Smith as his guardian in 1806.

SMITH, JOHN (tanner), father of John H. Smith in 1805 guardianship.

SMITH, JOHN (tanner), master of Samuel Row (son of Cornrod Row) in 1805 indenture.

SMITH, JOHN, age 18 on September 1, 1814, was indentured with the consent of his mother (not named) to Simon Furze [Turze?], of Baltimore County, in 1815 to learn to be a mason.

SMITH, JOHN, age 9 on September 1, 1805. Court appointed Frances Smith as his guardian in 1806.

SMITH, JOHN H. (son of John Smith, tanner), no age given in 1805. Court appointed William W. Webster as his guardian in 1805.

SMITH, JONATHAN, master of Amos Curry (son of Ann Curry) in 1805

indenture.

SMITH, MARTHA, age 3 on July 1, 1802. Court appointed her mother, Martha Smith, as her guardian in 1802.

SMITH, MARTHA, mother and guardian of Samuel Griffith Smith, Freenetta Smith, and Martha Smith in 1802.

SMITH, MOSES G., master of Levi Johnson (Negro) in 1806 indenture.

SMITH, PACA, guardian of James Martha Phillips (daughter of Sarah Phillips) in 1812.

SMITH, REUBEN, master of Samuel Wilson (Colored) in 1824 indenture.

SMITH, SAMUEL GRIFFITH, age 7 on December 25, 1801. Court appointed his mother, Martha Smith, as his guardian in 1802.

SMITH, THOMAS, age 11 in July, 1808. Court appointed Isaac Wooley as his guardian in 1808.

SMITHSON, DANIEL, age 16 on April 1, 1805. Court appointed John Dooran as his guardian in 1805.

SMITHSON, DANIEL, father of William Smithson in 1805 guardianship.

SMITHSON, EDWARD, age 14 on November 25, 1804. Court appointed William Smithson (son of Daniel Smithson) as his guardian in 1805.

SMITHSON, EDWARD, age 16 on November 25, 1806, was indentured to William Wright in 1807 to learn to be a cabinet maker.

SMITHSON, EDWARD, age 16 on November 25, 1806. Court appointed Thomas Smithson as his guardian in 1807 (because William Smithson refused to serve in 1805).

SMITHSON, GABRIEL, age 13 on February 10, 1807. Court appointed Thomas Smithson as his guardian in 1807 since William Smithson refused in 1805.

SMITHSON, GABRIEL, age 11 on February 10, 1805. Court appointed William Smithson (son of Daniel Smithson) as his guardian in 1805.

SMITHSON, JOHN, age 19 on June 20, 1805. Court appointed William Smithson (son of Daniel Smithson) as his guardian in 1805.

SMITHSON, JOHN, age 19 on June 20, 1805, was indentured to John Devoe in 1805 to learn to be a house carpenter.

SMITHSON, LUTHER, age 15 on May 25, 1807. Court appointed Thomas Smithson as his guardian in 1807 since William Smithson refused in 1805.

SMITHSON, LUTHER, age 13 on May 25, 1805. Court appointed William Smithson (son of Daniel Smithson) as his guardian in 1805.

SMITHSON, THOMAS, age 20 on March 1, 1805. Court appointed John Dooran as his guardian in 1805.

SMITHSON, THOMAS, guardian of Edward Smithson, Luther Smithson, and Gabriel Smithson in 1807 (because William Smithson refused to serve in 1805).

SMITHSON, WILLIAM (son of Daniel Smithson), appointed guardian of Edward Smithson, Luther Smithson, and Gabriel Smithson in 1805, but he refused to serve. Court then appointed Thomas Smithson in in his place in 1807.

SNOWDY, MATTHEW, master of Henry Warfield in 1802 indenture.

SOLOMON (Negro son of Negro Rachel), age 5 in 1803, "his parents are out of the county," was indentured to William Bull in 1803 to learn to be a farmer.

SOLOMON (Negro), age 6 on March 14, 1811, was indentured to Dr. Thomas E. Bond in 1811 to learn to be a farmer.

SOPHIA (Negro), age about 10 in 1823, valued at $100, and formerly owned by William Calwell, deceased, in October, 1823.

SPENCE, JAMES (orphan), age 17 on October 20, 1804, was indentured to John Spotswood Peck & Company in 1805 to learn to be a tanner.

SPENCER, ANN R., age 13 on November 24, 1815. Court appointed Maulden G. Middleton as her guardian in 1816.

SPENCER, EMARLIA [EMAULIS?], age 11 on March 26, 1816. Court appointed Maulden G. Middleton as her guardian in 1816.

SPENCER, EMARRILLA, age 14 on March 20, 1819. Court appointed Mary Shackell as her guardian in 1819.

SPENCER, HUGH, age 17 on May 31, 1822, was indentured in 1822 [name of master not given in record] to learn to be a blacksmith.

SPENCER, MARY, age 7 on April 12, 1815, was indentured with the consent of her mother (not named) to James Fulton in 1815 to learn to do housework.

SPENCER, THOMAS, guardian of John Nabb and Elisha Nabb in 1811.

SPENCER, WILLIAM (orphan), age 15 on December 10, 1804, was indentured to Isaac Towson in 1805 to learn to be a cooper.

SPENCER, WILLIAM, master of Nicholas Baldwin in 1808 indenture.

SPICER, ABRAHAM, master of John Wesley Jeffrey in 1829 indenture.

ST. CLAIR, GEORGE, master of John Thompson in 1804 indenture.

ST. CLAIR, HANNAH, guardian of James St. Clair and William St. Clair in 1822.

ST. CLAIR, JAMES, age 12 in April, 1821. Court appointed Hannah St. Clair as his guardian in 1822.

ST. CLAIR, THOMAS, guardian of Patty Blaney in 1812.

ST. CLAIR, WILLIAM, master of Christy Swan (son of Elizabeth Swan) in 1805 indenture.

ST. CLAIR, WILLIAM, age 10 in July, 1821. Court appointed Hannah St. Clair as his guardian in 1822.

STALLION, SAMUEL, age 9 on May 29, 1803, was indentured to John McKenney with the consent of his mother, Rebecca Bradley, in 1803 to learn to be a winsor [sic] chair maker.

STALLIONS, ISAAC, age 11 on February 10, 1801, was indentured to Parker Gilbert, Jr. in 1801 to learn to be a taylor.

STALLIONS, SAMUEL (son of Rebecca Bradley), age 10 on May 29, 1804, was indentured to John Davey in 1804 to learn to be a boot and shoemaker.

STANDIFORD, CLAUDIUS, master of Jacob Norris in 1809 indenture.

STANSBURY, ISAAC, master of Barney Moore (orphan) in 1819 indenture.

STEEL, JOHN, master of William Mooberry in 1816 indenture.

STEELE, JOHN, master of Thomas How (son of William How) in 1809 indenture.

STEPHEN (Negro, illegitimate), age 4 on November 24, 1825, was indentured with the consent of his mother (not named) to William Worthington in 1826 to learn to be a farmer.

STEPHENS, JOSHUA, master of Robert Cantler in 1829 indenture.

STEPHENS, MILCHA (Mulatto), mother of Sarah Stephens (Negro) in 1818 indenture.

STEPHENS, SARAH (Negro child of Mulatto Milcha), age 6 on

September 15, 1817, was indentured to Capt. William Trager in 1818 to learn to do housework.

STEPHENSON, SAMUEL, guardian of Daniel Cooley, Corbin Cooley, Lawson Cooley, and Sarah Ann Cooley (children of Sarah Cooley) in 1808.

STERETT, JOHN, master of William Maran (orphan) in 1823 indenture.

STEVENS, JOSHUA, master of John Coye in 1828 indenture.

STEWART, BENNETT, master of Stephen Kimble in 1813 indenture.

STOCKDALE, JOHN (orphan), age 9 as of May 20, 1826, was indentured with the consent of his grandfather (not named) to John H. Wiggers in 1826 to learn to be a cooper.

STOKES, JOSEPH, master of James Ward and John Robinson in 1804 indentures.

STOKES, NAT (Negro, son of Rachel Stokes), "who was born free," age 8 years, 3 months and 28 days as of May 21, 1806, was indentured to Zephaniah Bailey in 1806 to learn to be a farmer.

STOKES, RACHEL (Negro), mother of Nat Stokes in 1806 indenture.

STRATTEN, JOHN, age 17 on September 8, 1817, was indentured to Howel Mitchell in 1818 to learn to be a farmer.

STREETT, ABRM., age 18 on November 12, 1814. Court appointed Thomas Streett as his guardian in 1815.

STREETT, DAVID, age 14 on November 29, 1814. Court appointed Thomas Streett as his guardian in 1815.

STREETT, GLEEN [sic], age 20 on July 11, 1815. Court appointed Thomas Streett as his guardian in 1815.

STREETT, HANNAH, age 10 on July 10, 1815. Court appointed Thomas Streett as her guardian in 1815.

STREETT, JAMIMA, guardian of Rachel Streett, Sarah Streett, and Samuel Streett in 1803.

STREETT, JOHN, age 8 on November 29, 1814. Court appointed Thomas Streett as his guardian in 1815.

STREETT, RACHEL, age 12 on April 13, 1802. Court appointed Jamima Streett as her guardian in 1803.

STREETT, ROBERT, age 12 on April 26, 1815. Court appointed Thomas Streett as his guardian in 1815.

STREETT, SAMUEL, age 2 on November 17, 1802. Court appointed Jamima Streett as his guardian in 1803.

STREETT, SARAH, age 9 on December 10, 1802. Court appointed Jamima Streett as her guardian in 1803.

STREETT, SHADRACK, master of Mulatto Fanny and Mulatto William in 1815 indentures.

STREETT, THOMAS, guardian of Gleen [sic] Streett, Abrm. Streett, David Streett, Robert Streett, Hannah Streett, and John Streett in 1815.

STRICKLEN, JACOB, age 10 on August 11, 1807, was indentured to James Orr in 1807 to learn to be a potter.

STRICKLEN, JOHN (orphan), age 7 on November 1, 1809, was indentured to James Orr in 1810 to learn to be a potter.

STRICKLEN, THEODOCEY (orphan), age 10 on January 6, 1810, was indentured to James Orr in 1810 to learn to be a potter.

STRONG, ELINOR E., age 11 on July 4, 1802. Court appointed Jeremiah Biddison as her guardian in 1803.

STRONG, ELINOR ELIZABETH, no age given in 1802. Court appointed

Joseph Strong as her guardian in 1802.

STRONG, JOSEPH, father of Maximilian Strong in 1820 indenture.

STRONG, JOSEPH, guardian of William Strong and Elinor Elizabeth Strong in 1802.

STRONG, MAXIMILIAN (son of Joseph Strong), no age given in August, 1820, was indentured to William Bradford, of Abingdon, Maryland, in 1820 to learn to be a hatter.

STRONG, WILLIAM, age 16 on April 1, 1803. Court appointed Jeremiah Biddison as his guardian in 1803.

STRONG, WILLIAM, no age given in 1802. Court appointed Joseph Strong as his guardian in 1802.

STUMP, ANN (daughter of Elizabeth and Harman Stump, deceased), age 4 in 1802. Court appointed John Stump as her guardian with the consent of her mother Elizabeth Stump, widow, in 1802.

STUMP, ELIZABETH (daughter of Elizabeth and Harman Stump, deceased), age 8 on May, 1802. Court appointed John Stump as her guardian with the consent of her mother Elizabeth Stump, widow, in 1802.

STUMP, ELIZABETH, widow of Harman Stump and mother of Elizabeth Stump, Hannah Stump, Mary Stump, Ann Stump, and Harman Stump in 1802.

STUMP, HANNAH (daughter of Elizabeth and Harman Stump, deceased), age 7 in September, 1802. Court appointed John Stump as her guardian with the consent of her mother Elizabeth Stump, widow, in 1802.

STUMP, HARMAN (son of Elizabeth and Harman Stump, deceased), age 2 in 1802. Court appointed John Stump as his guardian with the consent of his mother Elizabeth Stump, widow, in 1802.

STUMP, HARMAN, husband of Elizabeth Stump and deceased father of Elizabeth Stump, Hannah Stump, Mary Stump, Ann Stump, and Harman Stump in 1802.

STUMP, HENRY, father of John Stump in 1812 and 1816 records.

STUMP, HENRY JR., master of Negro Isabella in 1807 indenture.

STUMP, HERMAN (son of John Stump), age 17 on August 13, 1815. Court appointed John Stump (son of Henry Stump) as his guardian in 1816.

STUMP, JOHN (son of Henry Stump), guardian of John Henry Price, Rachel Price, and Margaret Ann Price in 1812 with the consent of their mother (not named).

STUMP, JOHN (son of Henry Stump), guardian of Herman Stump (son of John Stump) in 1816.

STUMP, JOHN, father of Herman Stump in 1816 indenture.

STUMP, JOHN, guardian of Elizabeth Stump, Hannah Stump, Mary Stump, Ann Stump, and Harman Stump (children of Elizabeth and Harman Stump, deceased) in 1802.

STUMP, MARY (daughter of Elizabeth and Harman Stump, deceased), age 5 in 1802. Court appointed John Stump as her guardian with the consent of her mother Elizabeth Stump, widow, in 1802.

STUMP, SAMUEL C., master of Abraham Wright and Margarett Wright in 1825 indenture.

STUMP, SAMUEL C., master of John Miller in 1827 indenture.

STUMP, THOMAS C., master of Charles H. Bowser (Negro) in 1826 indenture.

STUMP, THOMAS C., master of William Rigby (Negro) in 1829 indenture.

STUMP, THOMAS C., master of Richard Miller in 1827 indenture.

STUMP, WILLIAM, master of Gabriel Dorsey and John Dorsey (sons of Josias Dorsey) in 1821 indentures.

SUKEY (Negro), age 8 on November 30, 1808, was indentured to Hezekiah Harryman in 1808 to learn to do housework.

SUSANNAH (Negro daughter of Negro Grace), "illegitimate child of color," age 2 years and 2 months in April, 1809, was indentured to William Dallam in 1809 to learn to do housework.

SUTTON, MARTHA, wife of Samuel Sutton in 1821 guardianship.

SUTTON, SAMUEL AND MARTHA (his wife), guardians of Frances Priscilla Drew in 1821.

SWAN, CHRISTY (son of Elizabeth Swan), age 6 on July 28, 1805, was indentured to William St. Clair in 1805 to learn to be a farmer.

SWAN, ELIZABETH, mother of Christy Swan and Frederic Swan in 1805 indenture.

SWAN, FREDERIC (son of Elizabeth Swan), age 8 on October 23, 1805, was indentured to George Carsins in 1805 to learn to be a farmer.

SWART, DAVID, master of Negro Sarah in 1829 indenture.

SWART, EPHRAIM, age 10 on October 4, 1814 [sic], was indentured with the consent of his father (not named) to Upton Reed and Rees Davis, cutlers, in 1813 to learn to be a shovel and spade maker.

SWART, EPHRAIM, master of Moses Hill in 1817 indenture.

SWART, EPHRAIM, master of John Henry in 1809 indenture.

SWART, EPHRAIM, master of William Jones in 1807 indenture.

SWART, EPHRAIM, master of Benjamin Debrular (orphan) in 1803 indenture.

SWARTH, GEORGE (son of Samuel Swarth), age 13 on July 2, 1812, was indentured to James Orr in 1812 to learn to be a potter.

SWARTH, SAMUEL, father of George Swarth in 1812 indenture.

TALBOTT, BOB (Negro son of Negro Ned and Esther Talbott), age 13 on July 8, 1805, was indentured to John Moughhan in 1805 to learn to be a cooper.

TALBOTT, ELIZABETH (Negro daughter of Esther Talbott), age 11 on August 10, 1806, was indentured to John Spotswood Peck in 1806 to learn to do housework.

TALBOTT, ESTHER (Negro), wife of Ned Talbott (Negro) and mother of Bob Talbott and Ned Talbott in 1805 indenture.

TALBOTT, ESTHER (Negro), wife of Ned Talbott (Negro) and mother of Elizabeth Talbott in 1806 indenture.

TALBOTT, NED (Negro son of Negro Ned and Esther Talbott), age 12 on March 10, 1805, was indentured to Thomas A. Hayes in 1805 to learn to be a farmer.

TALBOTT, NED (Negro), father of Elizabeth Talbott in 1806 indenture.

TALBOTT, NED (Negro), father of Bob Talbott and Ned Talbott in 1805 indenture.

TASSEY [PASSEY?], WILLIAM, no age given in 1820, was indentured with the consent of his father (not named) to Joseph Whitson in 1820 to learn to be a blacksmith.

TATE, DAVID, master of Negro Harriett, Negro Sharlotte, and Negro Benjamin in 1808 indentures.

TAYLOR, ASHBERRY, age 1 on February 25, 1812. Court appointed
Frances Taylor as his guardian in 1812.
TAYLOR, BENNETT, master of George W. Santee in 1816 indenture.
TAYLOR, CATHARINE, age 6 on October 4, 1811. Court appointed
Frances Taylor as her guardian in 1812.
TAYLOR, FRANCES, guardian of Otho Taylor, Sylvester Taylor, James
Taylor, Henry Taylor, Catharine Taylor, and Ashberry Taylor in
1812.
TAYLOR, HENRY, age 7 on October 24, 1811. Court appointed Frances
Taylor as his guardian in 1812.
TAYLOR, ISAIAH, guardian of Alce [sic] Meeks, Charlotte Meeks,
and William Meeks in 1810.
TAYLOR, JAMES, age 9 on October 4, 1811. Court appointed Frances
Taylor as his guardian in 1812.
TAYLOR, JAMES, master of James Packwood (orphan) in 1809
indenture.
TAYLOR, JAMES, master of James Shoady in 1801 indenture.
TAYLOR, JAMES, master of Negro Lewis in 1806 indenture.
TAYLOR, JAMES, see "Thrift, James (alias Taylor)," q.v., in 1816.
TAYLOR, JOSEPH EVEREST, age 14 on March 14, 1820, was indentured
with the consent of his mother (not named) to George
Crevensten in 1820 to learn to be a blacksmith.
TAYLOR, NELLY (Negro), mother of Sarah Taylor in 1829 indenture.
TAYLOR, OTHER, age 17 on July 6, 1813, was indentured with the
consent of his mother (not named) to Robert Miller in 1814 to
learn to be a boot and shoemaker.
TAYLOR, OTHO, age 15 on July 2, 1811. Court appointed Frances
Taylor as his guardian in 1812.
TAYLOR, RICHARD, guardian of Ann Maria Courtney in 1801.
TAYLOR, ROBERT, master of Aquila Ayres (alias Davison) in 1802
indenture.
TAYLOR, SARAH (freeborn Negro daughter of Nelly Taylor), age 18
on March 16, 1839 [1829?], was indentured to James C. Doddrell
on May 11, 1829 [to learn to be a servant?].
TAYLOR, SYLVESTER, age 12 on January 24, 1812. Court appointed
Frances Taylor as his guardian in 1812.
TAYLOR, THOMAS (ship carpenter), master of Negro Ben in 1803
indenture.
TAYLOR, WILLIAM, master of John Green and Negro Matilda in 1818
indenture.
TAYSON, CASSANDRA (illegitimate child), age 6 in November, 1809,
was indentured to Dorothy Johnson in 1810 to learn to do
housework.
TAYSON, ELIJAH (orphan), age 10 in August, 1808, was indentured
to Samuel Marshall in 1808 to learn to be a farmer.
TAYSON, MARY ANN (orphan), age 9 in June, 1809, was indentured to
Dorothy Johnson in 1810 to learn to do housework.
THOMAS (Negro), age 9 on September 1, 1802, was indentured to
James McGaw in 1803 to learn to be a cooper.
THOMAS, HANNAH (daughter of John and Mary Thomas), age 14 on June
24, 1805. Court appointed William Pyle as her guardian in
1806.
THOMAS, HARMON, master of Joseph Madden in 1823 indenture.
THOMAS, JAMES (son of John and Mary Thomas), age 17 on January
31, 1805. Court appointed William Pyle as his guardian in

1806.

THOMAS, JOHN (Colored, son of Samuel Thomas), no age given in 1828, was indentured with consent of his father to James Logue on April 12, 1828, for 4 years to learn to be a farmer.

THOMAS, JOHN (son of John and Mary Thomas), age 11 on June 13, 1805. Court appointed William Pyle as his guardian in 1806.

THOMAS, JOHN, father of James Thomas, Hannah Thomas, John Thomas, and William Thomas in 1806 guardianship.

THOMAS, LUDA (Negro daughter of Negro Ann Turner), "will be age 18 on March 15, 1810," was indentured to John Spottswood Peck in 1803 to learn to do housework.

THOMAS, MARY, wife of John Thomas and mother of James Thomas, Hannah Thomas, John Thomas, and William Thomas in 1806 guardianship.

THOMAS, SAMUEL, father of John Thomas (Colored) in 1828 indenture.

THOMAS, WILLIAM (son of John and Mary Thomas), age 9 in April, 1805. Court appointed William Pyle as his guardian in 1806.

THOMPSON, CHARLES (son of William Thompson), no age given in September, 1811, was indentured to John Anderson in 1811 to learn to be a cooper.

THOMPSON, EDWARD, master of Abram Bradford in 1828 indenture.

THOMPSON, ELIZABETH, age 12 on February 2, 1801, was indentured to Rolen and Jane Rogers in 1801 to learn to do housework.

THOMPSON, JAMES, age 16 in July, 1821. Court appointed Jebez Kirkwood as his guardian in 1822.

THOMPSON, JAMES, master of Danby Cody (Negro boy) in 1808 indenture.

THOMPSON, JOHN (son of Margaret Thompson), age 7 on June 9, 1804, was indentured to George St. Clair in 1804 to learn to be a weaver and farmer.

THOMPSON, JOHN, age 8 on December 30, 1817. Court appointed Henry Scarff as his guardian in 1818, and then John Kean in 1821.

THOMPSON, JOHN, age 14 on December 29, 1823, was indentured with the consent of his mother (not named) to Joseph Whitson in 1823 to learn to be a blacksmith.

THOMPSON, SUSAN, age 10 on February 14, 1818. Court appointed Henry Scarff as her guardian in 1818, and then John Kean in 1821.

THRIFT, JAMES (alias TAYLOR), "an illegitimate orphan," age 17 in September, 1816, was indentured to Joseph D. Parsons in 1816 to learn to be a blacksmith.

THRIFT, RICHARD, master of Edward Perry Carroll in 1807 indenture.

TIMMONS, COPELAND, age 19 on March 16, 1809. Court appointed Aaron Hill as his guardian in 1809.

TIMMONS, EDWARD, guardian of Providence Cord in 1816.

TODD, NANCY (daughter of Patrick Todd), age 16 on September 20, 1808, was indentured to Jonas Barecroft on February 27, 1800, to learn to read the Bible and to write.

TOLLEY, JAMES W., guardian of Thomas G. Howard, Eliza M. Howard, Ann M. Howard, Susan Howard, and James T. Howard in 1811.

TOM (Negro), age 12 on July 12, 1811, was indentured to Dr. Thomas E. Bond in 1811 to learn to be a farmer.

TOOGOOD, WILLIAM, see "Twogood (Toogood), William," q.v., in

1803.

TOUCHSTONE, DEBORAH, mother of Henry Touchstone in 1822 guardianship.

TOUCHSTONE, HENRY (son of Deborah and Henry Touchstone, deceased), age 16 on July 12, 1822. Court appointed John Touchstone as his guardian in 1822.

TOUCHSTONE, HENRY, deceased father of Henry Touchstone in 1822 guardianship.

TOUCHSTONE, JOHN, guardian of Henry Touchstone in 1822.

TOWER (Negro, illegitimate), age 10 on April 15, 1822, was indentured with the consent of his mother (not named) to John Magness in 182 to learn to be a tanner.

TOWER (Negro), age 16 in January, 1809, was indentured to Andrew Martin in 1809 to learn to be a farmer.

TOWNSLEY, JAMES (orphan), age 17 on September 8, 1808, was indentured to Benjamin Mahan in 1808 to learn to be a cooper.

TOWNSLEY, JAMES, age 10 on September 28, 1801. Court appointed John Mahon, Sr. as his guardian in 1802.

TOWNSLEY, JOHN, age 15 on October 9, 1801. Court appointed John Mahon, Sr. as his guardian in 1802.

TOWNSLEY, JOHN, age 15 on October 8, 1801, was indentured with the consent of his mother (not named) to Amos Evans in 1802 to learn to be a plasterer, painter and glazier.

TOWNSLEY, JOSEPH, age 13 on March 5, 1802. Court appointed John Mahon, Sr. as his guardian in 1802.

TOWNSLEY, JOSEPH, age 13 in 1802, was indentured to John Luckie in 1802 to learn to be a hat maker.

TOWNSLEY, WILLIAM, age 7 on September 26, 1801. Court appointed John Mahon, Sr. as his guardian in 1802.

TOWSON, ISAAC, master of William Wilcocks in 1804 indenture.

TOWSON, ISAAC, master of William Spencer (orphan) in 1805 indenture.

TOWSON, ISAAC, master of William How and John How (sons of William How) in 1801 indenture.

TOWSON, JOHN (son of Charles Towson), age 21 on February 8, 1808 [sic], was indentured with the consent of his father to David Hanway in 1803 to learn to be a miller.

TRAGER, WILLIAM (Captain), master of Sarah Stephens (Negro) in 1818 indenture.

TRAGER, WILLIAM (Captain), master of guardian of William Meeks in 1820 indenture.

TRAPLIN, WILLIAM (orphan), age 9 on August 9, 1822, was indentured to Nathan L. Bemis in 1823 to learn to be a miller.

TREDWAY, JAMES, master of John Brooks in 1815 indenture.

TREDWAY, THOMAS, master of Negro Isaac in 1808 indenture.

TRIMBLE, JOSEPH, master of Margaret Ann Beaton in 1830 indenture.

TUCKER, DAVID, master of Joanna Bodden in 1820 indenture.

TUCKER, JOHN, master of Richard Hawkins and Gerrard Bailey in 1811 indentures.

TURK, GEORGE, age 17 in June, 1810, was indentured with the consent of his parents (not named) to James Greenfield in 1810 to learn to be a carpenter.

TURNER, ANN (Negro), mother of Luda Thomas (Negro) in 1803 record.

TURNER, WILLIAM (orphan), age 16 on January 19, 1820, was

indentured to Washington Hanway in 1820 to learn to be a
fuller and dyer.

TURZE [FURZE?], SIMON (of Baltimore County), master of John Smith
in 1815 indenture.

TWOGOOD [TOOGOOD], WILLIAM (son of Sarah Twogood), age 3 years
and 9 months in March, 1803, was indentured to William
Robinson in 1803 to learn to be a cooper.

VANSICKLE, BENNETT, age 14 on January 13, 1802. Court appointed
Aquila Nelson as his guardian in 1802.

VANSICKLE, HENRY, guardian of John Chauncey in 1809.

WALKER, CORNELIUS (of Baltimore County), master of Baker Beavin
(son of Charles Beavin) in 1803 indenture.

WALKER, JAMES, father of Margaret Walker in 1812 indenture.

WALKER, MARGARET (daughter of James Walker), age 13 on June 13,
1813, was indentured to Richard and Ann Mansfield in 1812 to
learn to do housework.

WALLIS, JOHN JR. (of Baltimore County), master of Greenberry
Dorsey, Jr. in 1807 indenture.

WALLIS, WILLIAM, master of Negro Abraham in 1823 indenture.

WALLIS, WILLIAM, master of Richard Kenley (Negro) and Lewis
Kenley (Negro) in 1822 indentures.

WALTHAM, THOMAS (illegitimate son of Hannah Johnston), age 8
years and 11 months in December, 1822, was indentured to
Thomas Rickets in 1823 to learn to be a farmer.

WALTHOM, CHARLTON, age 20 in 1802. Court appointed William and
Sarah Chambers as his guardian in 1802.

WALTHOM, PHILAZANNA, age 10 in 1802. Court appointed William and
Sarah Chambers as her guardian in 1802.

WALTHOM, SARAH ELINA, age 12 in 1802 [same age as Thomas
Walthom]. Court appointed William and Sarah Chambers as her
guardian in 1802.

WALTHOM, THOMAS, age 12 in 1802 [same age as Sarah Elina
Walthom]. Court appointed William and Sarah Chambers as his
guardian in 1802.

WALTHOM, WILLIAM, age 5 in 1802, was indentured to William Sims
in 1802 to learn to be a blacksmith.

WALTHOM, WILLIAM, age 17 in 1802. Court appointed William and
Sarah Chambers as his guardian in 1802.

WALTON, JOHN (Colored, son of Lucy Walton), age 5 in March, 1830,
was indentured with the consent of his mother to Archabald
Henderson in 1830 to learn to be a farmer.

WALTON, LUCY (Negro), mother of John Walton in 1830 indenture.

WARD, JAMES, age 18 on July 8, 1804, was indentured to Joseph
Stokes in 1804 to learn to be a house carpenter.

WARD, JAMES, age 16 in 1802. Court appointed Joseph Robinson as
his guardian in 1802.

WARD, RICHARD, age 18 in 1802. Court appointed Joseph Robinson as
his guardian in 1802.

WARD, RICHARD, age 17 in 1802. Court appointed Barnett Johnson
(son of Barnett Johnson) as his guardian in 1802.

WARD, WILLIAM, age 15 in 1802. Court appointed Joseph Robinson as
his guardian in 1802.

WARFIELD, HENRY, age 17 on February 6, 1802, was indentured to
Mathew Snowdy in 1802 to learn to be a carpenter and joiner.

WARNER, JONATHAN, master of John Griffin (Negro) in 1829

indenture.

WARNER, MARY, age 2 on January 17, 1818. Court appointed Thomas and Jane Garrison as her guardian in 1818.

WARRICK, LEVINA (orphan), age 8 in September, 1808, was indentured to William Wright in 1809 to learn to do housework.

WASHINGTON (Negro), age 10 on April 15, 1816, was indentured with the consent of his mother (not named) to John Dever in 1816 to learn to be a farmer.

WASHINGTON, GEORGE (Negro), age 1 in September, 1819, was indentured with the consent of his mother (not named) to Samuel McConnell in 1820.

WASHINGTON, ROSANA, age 4 on April 25, 1824, "now in poor house," was indentured to Stephen Boyd in 1823 to learn to spin and sew.

WASKEY, CHRISTIAN, of Abingdon Town, Maryland, master of Caleb Parsons (Negro) in 1807 indenture.

WASKEY, ELIJAH, master of Isaac Garrett in 1814 indenture.

WASKEY, ELIJAH, master of Robert B. Sanders in 1813 indenture.

WASKEY, ELIJAH, see "Thomas Leastater (orphan)," q.v., in 1826.

WATERS, MARGARETT (daughter of Richard Waters), age 3 on May 12, 1816, was indentured to Samuel Hopkins in 1817 to learn to do housework.

WATERS, RICHARD, father of Margarett Waters in 1817 indenture.

WATKINS (Negro son of Negro Linda), age 11 on August 1, 1800, was indentured to Maurice Maulsby in 1801 to learn to be a blacksmith.

WATKINS, JAMES AND CATHARINE, masters of Elizabeth Harvey in 1811 indenture.

WATKINS, JOHN, master of Negro Aaron in 1815 indenture.

WATTERS, BENEDICT, age 14 in 1808. Court appointed Sarah F. Watters as his guardian in 1808.

WATTERS, CHARLES (Negro), master of Negro James in 1805 indenture.

WATTERS, ELIZABETH LESTER, age 4 in May, 1808. Court appointed Sally F. Watters as her guardian in 1808.

WATTERS, HENRY, age 8 on December 22, 1807. Court appointed Sally F. Watters as his guardian in 1808.

WATTERS, JACOB, age 5 on January 20, 1806, was indentured to David E. Price in 1806 to learn the milling business.

WATTERS, JOHN, age 16 in October, 1807. Court appointed Thomas H. Birckhead as his guardian in 1807.

WATTERS, JOHN, master of Henry Hill (Mulatto) in 1810 indenture.

WATTERS, JOSHUA (Negro), age 12 on February 10, 1820, was indentured with the consent of his father (not named) to Samuel Connelly in 1820 to learn to be a farmer.

WATTERS, JULIA ANN, age 6 in October, 1808. Court appointed Sally F. Watters as her guardian in 1808.

WATTERS, SALLY F., guardian of Benedict Watters, Henry Watters, Julia Ann Watters, and Elizabeth Lester Watters in 1808.

WAY, ISAAC (orphan), age 10 on April 3, 1811, was indentured to Daniel Harry in 1811 to learn to be a turner.

WAY, LEVERIDGE, age 9 years and 10 months in May, 1805, was indentured with the consent of his mother (not named) to Patrick McLaughlin in 1805 to learn to be a stone and bricklayer.

WEBSTER, CAROLINE, age 4 in April, 1802. Court appointed George
 Chauncey as her guardian in 1802.
WEBSTER, CASSANDRA (Negro daughter of Charles and Jane Webster),
 age 11 on February 15, 1809, was indentured to Mary Montgomery
 in 1809 to learn to do housework.
WEBSTER, CHARLES AND JANE (Negroes), parents of Cassandra Webster
 in 1809 indenture.
WEBSTER, CHAUNCEY, age 6 on December 25, 1801. Court appointed
 George Chauncey as his guardian in 1802.
WEBSTER, JOHN A. (Captain), master of Abraham Brooks in 1823
 indenture.
WEBSTER, JOHN A. (seaman), master of Isaac Aches in 1821
 indenture.
WEBSTER, JOSEPH (son of Samuel Webster), age 4 on February 4,
 1812. Court appointed Richard Webster as his guardian in 1812.
WEBSTER, MARY, mother of Susannah Webster in 1803 guardianship.
WEBSTER, RICHARD, age 9 on January 30, 1807. Court appointed
 Richard Webster, Jr. [Sr.?] as his guardian in 1807.
WEBSTER, RICHARD, guardian of Joseph Webster (son of Samuel
 Webster) in 1812.
WEBSTER, RICHARD JR. [SR.?], guardian of Richard Webster in 1807.
WEBSTER, RICHARD, master of William Gilmore in 1807 indenture.
WEBSTER, SAMUEL LEE, master of Negro John in 1817 indenture.
WEBSTER, SUSANNAH, age 15 in October, 1802. Court appointed her
 mother, Mary Webster, as her guardian in 1803.
WEBSTER, WILLIAM W., guardian of John H. Smith in 1805.
WEEKS, ANN, master of Negro Isaac in 1828 indenture.
WEEKS, DANIEL, master of Negro Harry in 1819 indenture.
WEEKS, JOHN SR., master of Moses Demby (Negro) in 1815 indenture.
WEEKS, SAMUEL (Negro, illegitimate), age 13 on November 16, 1828,
 was indentured to James C. Doddrell in 1829 to learn to be a
 farmer.
WELCH, WILLIAM, see "Botts, William (alias Welch)," q.v., in
 1809.
WEST, ANNE (daughter of Temperance Sinclair), age 12 on August
 10, 1806, was indentured to Alisanna Wilson in 1806 to learn
 to do housework.
WEST, DAVID (son of William West), age 8 years and 12 days on
 April 29, 1809, was indentured to Abraham Huff in 1809 to
 learn to be a cooper.
WEST, ENOS, master of Samuel Cook (son of Samuel Cook, of
 Baltimore County) in 1806 indenture.
WEST, ENOS, master of Eliza Dempsey (orphan) in 1804 indenture.
WEST, JOSHUA, age 6 in 1803, was indentured to James Amoss (son
 of William Amoss) in 1803 to learn to be a farmer.
WEST, THOMAS, master of Isaac Dempsey (orphan) in 1804 indenture.
WEST, WILLIAM (son of William West), age 14 years and 15 days on
 April 29, 1809, was indentured to Abraham Huff in 1809 to
 learn to be a cooper.
WEST, WILLIAM (son of William West, "not in the county"), age 9
 on April 1, 1804, was indentured to Simon Fitzgerald in 1804
 to learn to be a taylor.
WEST, WILLIAM, father of David West and William West in 1809
 indentures.
WEST, WILLIAM, father of William West in 1804 indenture.

WETHERALL, HENRY, age 19 on November 8, 1820, was indentured with the consent of his mother (not named) to William Bradford in 1820 to learn to be a hatter.

WETHERALL, HENRY, age 14 on November 8, 1815. Court recognized Charlotte Birckhead as his natural guardian in 1816.

WETHERALL, JAMES, age 18 on May 5, 1816. Court recognized Charlotte Birckhead as his natural guardian in 1816.

WETHERALL, MATTHEW, age 8 on March 23, 1816. Court recognized Charlotte Birckhead as his natural guardian in 1816.

WETHERALL, THOMAS G., age 17 years and 2 months in May, 1820, was indentured with the consent of his mother (not named) to Nathaniel ---[?]--- in 1820 to learn to be a hatter.

WETHERALL, THOMAS NICHOLSON G., age 13 on March 28, 1816. Court recognized Charlotte Birckhead as his natural guardian in 1816.

WETHERALL, WILLIAM, age 10 on March 10, 1816. Court recognized Charlotte Birckhead as his natural guardian in 1816.

WHEELER, ANNA, age 15 in July, 1808. Court appointed Henry G. Bussey as her guardian in 1809.

WHEELER, AUGUSTIN, age 10 on July 20, 1810. Court appointed Henry G. Bussey as his guardian in 1811.

WHEELER, BETSY, age 9 on January 22, 1811. Court appointed Henry G. Bussey as her guardian in 1811.

WHEELER, CHARITY TERESA, "born November 19, 1801." Court appointed Benjamin Green, Jr. as her guardian in 1802.

WHEELER, CHARLES, age 13 on June 9, 1810. Court appointed Henry G. Bussey as his guardian in 1811.

WHEELER, FRANCES, age 2 on October 2, 1801. Court appointed Benjamin Green, Jr. as her guardian in 1802.

WHEELER, HENRIETTA, master of Hannah Rhodes in 1801 indenture.

WHEELER, JAMES, age 13 in 1801, was indentured to Richard B. Dallam in 1801 to learn to be a farmer.

WHEELER, JAMES M., age 17 in November, 1821, was indentured with the consent of his guardian (not named) to Joshua Fulton in 1821 to learn to be a carpenter.

WHEELER, JAMES MITCHELL, age 7 on January 29, 1811. Court appointed Henry G. Bussey as his guardian in 1811.

WHEELER, JOHN F., master of Elizabeth Elliott in 1829 indenture.

WHEELER, JOSEPH, father of Richard Wheeler in 1804 indenture.

WHEELER, JULIAN, age 13 in June, 1808. Court appointed Henry G. Bussey as her guardian in 1809.

WHEELER, MICHAEL, age 5 on September 23, 1801. Court appointed Benjamin Green, Jr. as his guardian in 1802.

WHEELER, RICHARD (son of Joseph Wheeler), age 18 on October 8, 1804, was indentured with the consent of his father to Joshua Husband in 1804 to learn to be a tanner and currier.

WHEELER, SYLVESTER, age 19 on February 3, 1811. Court appointed Henry G. Bussey as his guardian in 1811.

WHITAKER, EMMALE, age 11 in October, 1810. Court appointed Benjamin Everist as her guardian in 1811.

WHITAKER, EVERIST, age 8 in March, 1811. Court appointed Benjamin Everist as his guardian in 1811.

WHITAKER, ISAAC, master of Richard Wilmer (Negro) in 1820 indenture.

WHITAKER, JOHN, age 18 in October, 1810. Court appointed Benjamin

Everist as his guardian in 1811.

WHITAKER, JOHN, age 16 years and 4 months on March 11, 1808, was indentured to Philip Bennet in 1808 to learn to be a cordwainer.

WHITAKER, JOHN S., master of Samuel Whiteford in 1804 indenture.

WHITAMORE, HENRY, master of Jane McNulty in 1829 indenture.

WHITE, JAMES, master of Cyrus Combest in 1806 indenture.

WHITEFORD, ARCHER R., age 9 on February 27, 1818. Court recognized Eliza D. Whiteford as his natural guardian in 1818.

WHITEFORD, CUNNINGHAM, master of Negro Lewis and Negro Charles (sons of Negro Sarah) in 1817 indentures.

WHITEFORD, DODRIGE S., age 6 on November 29, 1817. Court recognized Eliza D. Whiteford as his natural guardian in 1818.

WHITEFORD, ELIZA D., natural guardian of Mary R. Whiteford, Archer R. Whiteford, and Dodrige S. Whiteford in 1818.

WHITEFORD, MARY R., age 11 in May, 1817. Court recognized Eliza D. Whiteford as her natural guardian in 1818.

WHITEFORD, ROBERT (orphan), "age 12 or 13" in 1808, was indentured to John W. McComas in 1809 to learn to be a farmer and cooper.

WHITEFORD, SAMUEL (orphan), age 15 on June 7, 1810, was indentured to Francis Grupy in 1810 to learn to be a tanner and currier.

WHITEFORD, SAMUEL, age 9 on June 7, 1804, was indentured with the consent of his mother (not named), first to Elijah Fell to learn to be a miller and secondly to John S. Whitaker to learn to be a tanner in 1804.

WHITEFORD, WILLIAM, one of the guardians of Mary McKinnon, Michael McKinnon, Thomas McKinnon, and Rachel McKinnon in 1811.

WHITSON, JOSEPH, master of John Thompson in 1823 indenture.

WHITSON, JOSEPH, master of William Tassey [Passey?] in 1820 indenture.

WHITSON, JOSEPH, master of Robert Prewett in 1821 indenture.

WIGGERS, JOHN H., master of John Stockdale in 1826 indenture.

WIGGINS, JOSEPH, master of Thomas Loney and Mary Ann Loney (children of Alse and Amos Loney, deceased) in 1811 indentures.

WIGGINS, JOSEPH, master of Abraham Ditto (orphan) in 1805 indenture.

WILCOCKS, WILLIAM, age 17 on August 10, 1803, was indentured to Isaac Towson in 1804 to learn to be a cooper.

WILGIS, SUSANNAH, age 11 on March 20, 1808, was indentured with the consent of her father (not named) to John and Elizabeth Renshaw in 1808 to learn to do housework.

WILLIAM (Negro, illegitimate), age 6 on August 20, 1811, was indentured to Samuel Ricketts in 1811 to learn to be a farmer.

WILLIAM (Negro), age 18 in March, 1803, was indentured with the consent of his mother (not named) to Buckler Bond in 1803 to learn to be a farmer.

WILLIAMS, BENJAMIN (Colored, son of William Williams), age 13 in March, 1828, was indentured with the consent of his father to Oliver H. Amos in 1828 to learn to be a farmer.

WILLIAMS, JOHN (son of Martha Williams), no age given in 1804, was indentured to Walter T. Hall in 1804 to learn to be a merchant and book keeper.

WILLIAMS, JOHN JR., no age given in September, 1808, was indentured with the consent of his father (not named) to Charles Freeman in 1808 [trade not specified in the record].

WILLIAMS, MARTHA (Negro), by the will of Elizabeth Johnson in 1820, was freed in March, 1828.

WILLIAMS, RALPH (Colored, son of William Williams), age 7 on February 14, 1828, was indentured with the consent of his father to Oliver H. Amos in 1828 to learn to be a farmer.

WILLIAMS, WILLIAM (Colored), father of Ralph Williams and Benjamin Williams in 1828 indenture.

WILMER, JAMES, age 16 on November 4, 1809. Court appointed Merekin Bond as his guardian in 1810.

WILMER, JAMES M., age 18 on November 4, 1811. Court appointed James Bond Preston as his guardian in 1812.

WILMER, MARY JANE (Negro), age 7 on January 1, 1821, "abandoned by her parents," was indentured to Samuel McConnell in 1820 to learn to do housework.

WILMER, RICHARD (Negro), age 9 on January 1, 1821, "abandoned by his parents," was indentured to Isaac Whitaker in 1820 to learn to be a farmer.

WILMOTT, RUTH, by her 1812 will, freed George Ruff (Negro) in 1824.

WILSON, ALISANNA, master of Anne West (daughter of Temperance Sinclair) in 1806 indenture.

WILSON, AMY (Negro), mother of Ashbury Wilson (Negro) in 1807 indenture.

WILSON, ASHBURY (son of Negro Amy) "a child of color, free born," age 7 years, 3 months, and 10 days as of July 1, 1807, was indentured to Jacob Wilson (Negro), "a free man of color," to learn to be a miller.

WILSON, CHRISTOPHER, master of Henry Corde (Negro) in 1828 indenture.

WILSON, ISAIAH (Negro orphan), age 13 on February 1, 1828, was indentured to John O'Neil in 1828 to learn to be a nail and spike maker.

WILSON, JACOB (free Negro), master of Ashbury Wilson (Negro) in 1807 indenture.

WILSON, JAMES, age 5 on July 5, 1824. Court appointed William Irvin as his guardian in 1825.

WILSON, JAMES, master of Robert Montgomery in 1825 indenture.

WILSON, JOHN, age 20 on November 14, 1808. Court appointed Ruth Wilson as his guardian in 1809.

WILSON, JOHN, age 7 on January 11, 1825. Court appointed William Irvin as his guardian in 1825.

WILSON, LEE, age 17 on January 1, 1802, was indentured to Aquila McComas in 1802 to learn to be a house carpenter and joiner.

WILSON, LEE, age 18 in January, 1803. Court appointed his mother, Mary Wilson, as his guardian in 1803.

WILSON, MARY, age 11 in 1803. Court appointed her mother, Mary Wilson, as her guardian in 1803.

WILSON, MARY, master of Sarah Elizabeth Jane (Negro) in 1826 indenture.

WILSON, MARY, master of Sarah Deaver (daughter of Martha Deaver) in 1806 indenture.

WILSON, MARY, mother and guardian of Lee Wilson, Priscilla
Wilson, Samuel Wilson, and Mary Wilson in 1803.

WILSON, PRISCILLA, age 14 in 1803. Court appointed her mother,
Mary Wilson, as her guardian in 1803.

WILSON, RACHEL, age 19 in August, 1805. Court appointed William
Wilson, Esq., as her guardian in 1805.

WILSON, RUTH, guardian of John Wilson in 1809.

WILSON, SAMUEL (Colored), age 9 years and 3 months on July 13,
1824, was indentured with the consent of his mother (not
named) to Reuben Smith in 1824 to learn to be a farmer.

WILSON, SAMUEL, age 13 in 1803. Court appointed his mother, Mary
Wilson, as his guardian in 1803.

WILSON, SAMUEL, master of Robert Dobbin in 1830 indenture.

WILSON, SAMUEL, master of Josias Johnson in 1824 indenture.

WILSON, THOMAS, master of Walter Bradford (Negro) in 1814
indenture.

WILSON, WILLIAM (Esquire), guardian of Rachel Wilson in 1805.

WILSON, WILLIAM (silversmith), master of Rebecca Mackentire in
1802 indenture.

WILSON, WILLIAM, age 3 on September 22, 1824. Court appointed
William Irvin as his guardian in 1825.

WOOD, ELISHA, age 8 on January 1, 1815, was indentured to William
Miller in 1815 to learn to be a farmer.

WOOD, JOHN (son of James Wood), of Havre de Grace, Maryland,
master of David Ross in 1815 indenture.

WOOD, JOSHUA, master of Ebenezer Nowland in 1801 indenture.

WOODLAND, WILLIAM, master of Henry Bradford (Negro) in 1819
indenture.

WOODS, JOHN, age 16 on June 5, 1821, was indentured to Amos Lake
in 1821 to learn to be a wheelwright.

WOOLEY, ISAAC, guardian of Thomas Smith in 1808.

WOOLSEY, HENRY, master of Charity Chance (Mulatto) in 1804
indenture.

WORTHINGTON, CAROLINE ANNE, age 10 on May 18, 1823. Court
appointed William Worthington as her guardian in 1823.

WORTHINGTON, HANNAH, age 14 on March 12, 1823. Court appointed
William Worthington as her guardian in 1823.

WORTHINGTON, PRISCILLA, age 13 on September 28, 1823. Court
appointed William Worthington as her guardian in 1823.

WORTHINGTON, SAMUEL, master of Negro London in 1826 indenture.

WORTHINGTON, SUSANNAH, age 12 on December 16, 1823. Court
appointed William Worthington as her guardian in 1823.

WORTHINGTON, WILLIAM, guardian of Hannah Worthington, Priscilla
Worthington, Susannah Worthington, and Caroline Anne
Worthington in 1823.

WORTHINGTON, WILLIAM, guardian of Daniel L. Chew and Eliza
Cassandra Chew (children of Ann W. Chew) in 1820.

WORTHINGTON, WILLIAM, master of Negro John and Negro Stephen in
1826 indentures.

WORTHINGTON, WILLIAM, master of Negro John in 1822 indenture.

WRIGHT, ABRAHAM (son of Erastus Wright), age 14 years and 8
months as of July 9, 1825, was indentured to Samuel C. Stump
in 1825 to learn to be a farmer.

WRIGHT, ERASTUS, father of Abraham Wright and Margarett Wright in
1825 indenture.

WRIGHT, MARGARETT (daughter of Erastus Wright), age 13 years and 3 months as of July 9, 1825, was indentured to Samuel C. Stump in 1825 to learn to do housewifery.

WRIGHT, WILLIAM, (Negro)_, "no parents living," age 16 on April 21, 1822, was indentured to Samuel Bradford, Esq., in 1822 to learn to be a farmer.

WRIGHT, WILLIAM, master of Edward Smithson in 1807 indenture.

WRIGHT, WILLIAM, master of Levina Warrick (orphan) in 1809 indenture.

YORK, DANIEL (orphan), age 15 in 1808, was indentured to John Roberts in 1808 to learn to be a farmer.

YORK, ELIZABETH, age 13 on December 4, 1800. Court appointed William York as her guardian in 1801.

YORK, WILLIAM, guardian of Elizabeth York in 1801.

YORK, ZELFA, guardian of Sarah York Scott in 1803.

YOUNG, ALEXANDER, age 2 in December, 1805. Court appointed Archer Hays as his guardian in 1806.

YOUNG, ARCHER HAYS, age 8 in March, 1806. Court appointed Archer Hays as his guardian in 1806.

YOUNG, JOHN (son of Mary Young), age 16 on June 10, 1805, was indentured to Joshua Husbands in 1805 to learn to be a tanner.

YOUNG, JOHN, age 16 in June, 1805. Court appointed Archer Hays as his guardian in 1806.

YOUNG, MARY, mother of John Young in 1805 indenture.

YOUNG, ROBERT, age 12 in April, 1805. Court appointed Archer Hays as his guardian in 1806.

YOUNG, SARAH, age 10 in April, 1805. Court appointed Archer Hays as her guardian in 1806.

YOUNG, THOMAS JEFFERSON, age 5 in February, 1806. Court appointed Archer Hays as his guardian in 1806.

Other books by the author:

www.ingramcontent.com/pod-product-compliance
Lightning Source LLC
LaVergne TN
LVHW021541080426
835509LV00019B/2765